THE SEVEN DEADLY SINS?

THE SEVEN DEADLY SINS?

Issues in Clinical Practice and Supervision for Humanistic and Integrative Practitioners

Anne Kearns

KARNAC
LONDON   NEW YORK

First published in 2005 by
H. Karnac (Books) Ltd.
6 Pembroke Buildings, London NW10 6RE

British Library Cataloguing in Publication Data

A C.I.P. for this book is available from the British Library

ISBN: 1 85575 353 7

Edited, designed and produced by The Studio Publishing
Services Ltd, Exeter EX4 8JN

Printed in Great Britain by Hobbs the Printers Ltd, Totton, Hampshire

10 9 8 7 6 5 4 3 2 1

www.karnacbooks.com

Contents

Contents

CHAPTER EIGHT

*In memory of my mother, Regina, who told me never
to put anything in writing.
And for Penelope who was patient.*

About the author

Anne Kearns trained in psychoanalytic psychotherapy in the USA and in Transactional Analysis and Gestalt in the UK. She is a former Chair and Teaching and Supervising member of the Gestalt Psychotherapy & Training Institute. In 1999 she founded The Growing Edge, a consortium of psychotherapists and other professionals who are interested in the development of the profession of psychotherapy through post-qualification training and consultation. Anne has an MSc in Integrative Psychotherapy and was Course Director of the training in Integrative Group Therapy at the Metanoia Institute from 1994-1996 and a Primary Tutor on the Integrative Psychotherapy training from 1994-1999. With Penny Daintry (co-author of the chapters on 'Eating Disorders' and 'Shame'), she is the author of 'Shame in the supervisory relationship: living with the enemy' (*British Gestalt Journal*, 9(1), 2000). She is an academic adviser to the MSc in Gestalt Psychotherapy at the Metanoia Institute and teaches and supervises Gestalt and Integrative psychotherapists in the UK and abroad. Anne has a private practice in West London. At the moment she is completing her doctoral studies in the areas of post-qualification training and procedural ethics.

Introduction

In 1985, following eight years of three-times-a-week on the couch psychoanalysis and clutching a Masters of Science in Clinical Social Work from Columbia University, I came to live in London. An MSc in Social Work is one of the prerequisites to train as a psychoanalyst in New York State, and I wove my way through the two-year, full-time course being taught and supervised as much as possible by psychoanalysts and psychoanalytic psychotherapists. It was my intention to join their ranks. I arrived in London and headed almost immediately for the Tavistock to inquire about training there.

Fate intervened when I realized that I would first have to earn a living to pay for any training I intended to undertake. I went to work for an advertising agency and was sent on an 'Introduction to Transactional Analysis', or a TA 101, at a place in Ealing called Metanoia. I went on to train in TA and gestalt. For the past twelve years or so I have been teaching and supervising humanistic and integrative psychotherapists from various trainings around the country. I have also been thinking about the effectiveness of those training courses and some of that thinking will be reflected here.

The practice of psychoanalysis was traditionally passed down by key theorists to their prodigies. This was usually done informally, the aspiring analyst entering into a 'training analysis' with his mentor. Jung and Adler began their journeys as independent theorists by lying on Freud's couch. Guntrip has written critically of his analyses with Fairbairn and Winnicott. Fritz Perls, the founder of Gestalt Therapy, was analysed and supervised by several of Freud's disciples such as Horney, Deutsch, Reich, and Fenichel.

The persecution of the Jews before and during the Second World War brought many second- and third-generation psychoanalysts to America. Some, like Horney and Deutsch, remained true to their Freudian roots. Others, like Perls and Reich, created their own schools of psychotherapy by, in Perls's case, integrating strands of Freud, Reich, Gestalt psychology, existentialism and Zen. Eric Berne, a native North American, developed his Transactional Analysis (TA) as a sort of object relations with popular appeal and ready accessibility.

By the 1960s Perls was well established as a charismatic figure in a movement that Rowan (2001) calls the 'third force' – those therapies that developed in opposition to psychoanalysis and behaviourism. Berne's TA and Carl Rogers's Client Centred Therapy had also taken hold in a climate in post-war America that emphasized personal responsibility and self-expression.

Despite the recent trend that has seen most training courses that lead to UKCP registration through the Humanistic and Integrative Psychotherapy Section (HIPS) become routes to Masters degrees, there remains a sort of 'hangover' from the 1960s when catharsis and 'speaking one's truth' were valued above intellectualization and research. Trainees are required to 'be themselves' and to spontaneously interact with each other and the facilitator in a process group; to use each other to practise their therapeutic skills in smaller groups; and then to be available with their thinking intact to absorb whatever academic input the trainer has planned for the day. This format encourages trainees to regress and, at some level, to be unable to engage with the theory.

I believe that humanistic and integrative trainings, with their emphasis on the 'here and now', have ignored the 'shadow' at their peril and have produced psychotherapists who may be unequipped to recognize and intervene effectively in processes that enter the therapeutic encounter from the client's and therapist's historical, developmental, and personal 'field'.

It was through my work as a supervisor of nearly or newly qualified psychotherapists that the seed for what became a post-qualification training course called 'The Seven Deadly Sins?' was sown. My supervisees and I came to see that there had been a number of areas or themes – diagnosis, schizoid phenomena, addiction, envy, shame, eating disorders, and trauma – that kept arising in their practice that had been under-discussed (or not covered at all) in their original training. I began to refer to these as 'The Seven Deadly Sins?'. I also began to be interested in how so much of what we describe in our clinical discussions of fragile self-process and the transference relationship was twentieth century language for what our forebears would have described as sin and possession.

This book is my attempt to condense some of what I and my colleagues, Penny Daintry, Joy Appleby, Diane Hodgson, and Mike Lawley have taught on 'The Seven Deadly Sins?'. Having said that, the opinions expressed in the pages to follow are at times controversial and they are mine alone. What follows is my attempt to make more accessible some concepts from the world of psychoanalysis, self-psychology, and affective neuroscience, as well as to comment on some of the challenges of working 'in the real world' when supported by a humanistically orientated training and philosophy. I am addressing humanistic practitioners as well as their supervisors. The first chapter, 'The sorcerer's apprentice' is aimed more at supervisors, but should be of interest to the clinician as a way of reflecting on the experience of training and on the assumptions made as a result. Chapters Four–Eight focus on issues in clinical practice and in supervision, with the chapter on shame focusing on shame in the supervisory relationship. That chapter, and the one on eating disorders, were written in collaboration with my colleague and partner, Penny Daintry, and have appeared in other forms elsewhere. Much of the book relies on examples from my clinical practice. In Chapter Four I have used a rather lengthy example of my work with a client that I have called Ruth to illustrate how I worked with what some might see as an addictive problem. I also refer to Ruth in other chapters to show how it is possible to look at the same clinical presentation through different lenses.

Although the book follows a sort of logical order, it should also be possible for the reader to read one chapter without having read any of the others.

I describe myself as an integrative psychotherapist, by which I mean specifically that I use both an object relations and humanistic–existentialist approach to my work. Humanistic therapists often are put off by the word 'object'. To me it just refers to a different kind of human relating that belongs more to the past than to the present. An 'object' is an aspect of a past relationship that is internalized by the client and experienced as though it were an aspect of the therapist or of himself. Fairbairn, who I believe did much to 'humanize' psychoanalytic thinking, was an object relations theorist. He pointed out that people seek other people as opposed to the pleasure that Freud originally thought we were after. Even Freud came eventually to describe transference as the patient's way of living his love. I like that, and it has supported me through some pretty difficult times when it feels as if there is anything *but* love in the room.

As much as I believe in psychotherapy, am interested in the theory and ever-fascinated and challenged by the practice, after twenty-something years of being a client and a therapist I can honestly say that I'm not sure that the therapeutic relationship is any more effective than other kinds of relationships. Oddly enough it is my uncertainty that keeps me going. I am grateful to my clients and supervisees, who have let me learn from them some of what I share with you here.

I want to acknowledge those who taught me as well as those who have given me opportunities to supervise and teach: Oliver McShane, Joseph Simo, Louise Engel, Senta Driver, the late Sue Fish, Petruska Clarkson, Maria Gilbert, Talia Levine Bar-Yoseph, Gaie Houston, Peter Philippson, Margot Sunderland, Joanna Beazley-Richards, and Lynda Osborne.

I am grateful, too, to all 'Deadly Sinners' past and present. You know who you are. Finally, I want to thank Joy Appleby, Julie Fry, Tracy Goodman, Donna Hayward-Sussex, Mike Lawley, Susi Noble, Marysia Renshaw, Paul Hitchings, Jacky Selwyn-Smith, and Andri White for their contributions; Karen Mahl who was always on the end of a phone; and Dinah Ashcroft and Marie Adams for their editorial help and warm encouragement.

It is my hope that dipping into this book will inspire the reader to explore some of the writers who have had an impact on my work. They have been marked with asterisks in the bibliography.

'It was a good life being an existentialist, although not too good for all the other, non-existentialist people around one.'

A. McCall Smith, *Morality for Beautiful Girls*

'The psychotherapist is the true successor of the exorcist. His business is not to pronounce the forgiveness of sins but to cast out devils.'

W. R. D. Fairbairn (1986)

'Teach us to care and not to care. Teach us to sit still.'

T. S. Eliot, *Ash Wednesday*

CHAPTER ONE

THE SORCERER'S APPRENTICE

The main challenge for me, as a supervisor of emerging psychotherapists, is to teach the theoretical and practical aspects of a psychotherapy that is based on the intentional use of relationship to people who may have had very little experience of clinical relationship, either as therapists or as clients. The paradox is that most of the relational issues addressed in the training are the very ones that the majority of trainees are struggling with for the first time, not just as beginning clinicians but, often, as beginning clients.

It is not unusual for entry-level psychotherapy trainees to have had no previous clinical experience or personal therapy. These trainees look to the outside for learning and may also have limitations in ego development that will affect their growth as a therapist. (Stoltenberg & Delworth, 1987). Trainees at this level tend to focus on the client rather than on themselves and, when they do focus on their own experience, it tends to be as a result of 'performance anxiety' and does not usually lead to clinically useful self-awareness. I have found it particularly stretching of myself as a trainer to help trainees to see that having 'negative' feelings such as irritation and exasperation towards a client does not necessarily indicate a flaw in the therapist's character but, rather, can be a form of communication from or about the client.

Even those more clinically experienced trainees still have difficulty in '. . . separating useful responses to a client that are based on accurate perceptions of the client's interpersonal interactions from countertransference[1] issues that are effectively blocked from awareness.' (*ibid.*, p. 76). Trainees at this level often over-identify with the client and will resist diagnostic and assessment techniques. This over-identification with the client also often gets in the way of trainees appreciating that there *are* differences between people, not just in their personality structures, but also in their gender and socio-cultural identities.

It has been my experience that trainees who have not yet successfully separated from their families of origin or from their children will also resist developmental theories and their clinical application. A supervisor of beginning psychotherapists must find a way to deliver diagnostic and child development models in a way that is 'palatable'; that is to say, that is respectful of the very strong possibility that the trainees will personalize this material and will use it to find themselves in some way deficient. They may take an oppositional position and hold the polarity of 'political correctness' as a deflection from any real learning. I want my supervisees to learn to be interested in and excited by their awareness of difference rather than to see it as a failure of empathy.

Helping trainees to reach a clinical understanding of empathy or its first cousin, inclusion, also has its challenges, as many 'beginners' view the clinician's role as necessarily warm and empathic and often see constructive confrontation as, as one trainee frequently put it, 'being horrible to people'. Beginners also tend to have an aversion to interpretation and fervently believe that humanistic therapists don't interpret. They do. They just call it something else. In gestalt, the therapist offers an 'interpretation' by saying, 'My hunch is that . . .'. A person-centred therapist might say, 'I don't know if this fits for you but I have a strong sense that . . .'. Call it what you will, what gives interpretation by any other name its humanistic credentials is that it is 'offered' as a possibility, not handed down as the official version of the truth.

Beginners also tend to be wary of theory as limiting of the therapist and diagnosis as depersonalizing of the client. My task as a supervisor is to help them to see that theory and diagnosis are ways of organizing and making sense of their thinking and emotional responses rather than pejorative reifications or instruments of power; to see that each clinical intervention involves an awareness of self and other and is *choiceful* rather than creative or prescribed.

I believe that supervisors of emerging therapists must take as a working assumption that psychotherapists often function within a narcissistic system where we can only value ourselves when our achievements meet our rather high expectations of ourselves. Yontef (1993) has said about narcissists that,

> . . . they do not assume that struggle is normal, do not assume they should have to struggle and do not feel a confident and loving feeling toward themselves as they go through the pain that is involved in learning. [p. 435]

He also reminds us that trainees tend to feel shame when they become aware of what they do not yet know. The supervisor of beginning psychotherapists must be mindful of the potential for shame in the supervisory relationship (see Chapter Seven) and, at the same time, must not treat the trainees as if they are too fragile to face themselves and their own limitations and deficits head-on. I must always struggle to find a balance between recognizing a trainee's real limitations and challenging him to move to a new place of knowing without pushing him into a 'narcissistic trap' of believing that he is brilliant on the one hand or hopeless on the other. A sense of humour helps.

Above all I attempt to approach my task with the knowledge that I was once a client and a trainee. I hope that I can share what I know and who I am, including the mistakes I have made and something about my own therapeutic journey. I have found that if I can come to this work supported by the memories of my own continuing journey to becoming a psychotherapist, including the challenges that I no doubt presented to my trainers and therapists, then I am less likely to pathologize and infantilize the trainees and more likely to model acceptance of self – warts and all – and, in doing so, to create an environment where staying with one's confusion and 'not knowing' is as valued as is moving towards conscious clinical competence.

Challenging dogma

There would appear to be two types of humanistic and integrative therapists practising in the UK today – those who, like me, learned a first language and, when that language was no longer effective in explaining what we were experiencing as human beings or as practitioners, learned another. And another. The second type is the single school practitioner who has learned a first language and is sticking to it. Even integrative psychotherapy – as if there were any agreement about what that is – is now being taught as a first language. Speaking as someone who has taught and supervised integrative psychotherapists

from different trainings, my experience is that by attempting to teach many languages at once, or to teach a meta-
language, we have failed to lay a secure foundation and
may be producing anxious therapists. If I think about my
experience supervising integrative trainees I have observed
that those who came to integration after having learned a
first 'psychotherapeutic' language are less anxious practitioners and are more able to deal with complexity, ambi-
guity, and inconsistency and to tolerate and to learn from
their mistakes – or failures.

So often, when I sit as a supervisor with someone who
does support one way of thinking about and working with
human experience above all others, or who is surprised
that a concept central to their 'language' is shared by or
even originated in another, I'm reminded of the joke
about the guy who dies and goes to heaven. He's met by
the gatekeeper who asks, 'Religion?'

'None', says the guy.

The gatekeeper looks at his list and says, 'Let me see
. . . agnostic . . . atheist . . . that'll be rooms 4–21. Come
with me.'

So, the guy follows him down a seemingly endless
corridor with numbered doors. Behind one door he hears
muffled speech and clinking glasses.

'Who's in there?', he asks the gatekeeper.

'That'll be the C of E. They like to have sherry parties.'

They continue until they come to a door behind which
can be heard ecstatic laughter.

'Who's in there?', the guy asks.

'Those are the Buddhists', says the gatekeeper (mildly
irritated) to the guy who keeps asking questions as they
walk down the corridor. 'Look', says the gatekeeper, 'I
really appreciate your curiosity but I'm going to have to

ask you to be very quiet when we get down to that next set of doors.'

'Why?', says the guy.

'Because', says the gate keeper (whispering), 'that's where the Catholics are and they don't think anyone else is here.'

One challenge as a supervisor of 'single school' trainees is to help them to see that theories are no more than stories that we tell to explain what makes people tick; that no theory is more 'true' than another – just more compatible with a therapist's personal and historical experience and perspective. It is also a challenge to help trainees to see that concepts such as 'commitment', 'confidentiality', and the 'core conditions' are ideals rather than absolutes. I am being deliberately irreverent because I have too often seen therapists suffer from burn-out as a result of the high expectations they put on themselves to be respectful of their clients at all times.

When I was a trainee in New York, I worked in a unit that provided short- and long-term therapy to municipal employees and their families. Two of the cultural norms that I have embraced from those days are versions of what management referred to as 'the padded cell' and 'mental health days'. The padded cell was a spare room in the unit where we were encouraged to go with a colleague when we had heard particularly troubling stories during an intake interview. Frequently gales of laughter could be heard coming out of the padded cell as one therapist 'debriefed' another, using humour to diffuse the horrors of many tales from the city. I used to call it the 'MASH syndrome'. Far from being cruel and intolerant, debriefing like this helped me and my colleagues to be *more* available to hear stories that were out of our range of experience.

All staff in the unit – therapists, managers and recep-
tionists – were also *required* to take a day off every six
weeks whenever they felt like it. This did not have to be
arranged in advance, nor did we have to feign illness in an
early morning phone call. We just phoned in and said,
'I'm taking a mental health day.' While I don't recom-
mend such spontaneity in private practice, I do support
my supervisees and colleagues to take planned mental
health days. When supervisees are over-loaded with life
stressors such as family illness or bereavement I require it.

Deconstructing myths

As a supervisor and as a therapist's therapist, I am interested in the myths that come to be believed by members
of the profession.

I remember spending a few days when I was a trainee
with Claude Steiner, who was well-known in the TA
world for – among other things – his 'no suicide contract'.
A member of the group presented a client for supervision.
The client was a successful professional in his fifties,
married to the same person for twenty-something years,
who had come into therapy because he was finding
himself thinking more and more about leaving his job in
the City and moving to the country to paint. He was
interested in exploring the meaning of this fantasy at this
stage in his life before he shared it with his wife and children. The therapist gave this history and presenting 'problem' and then said that she was careful to get the client to
agree to a 'no-suicide' contract. Steiner replied in genuine
amazement, 'What on earth for?!' The eager-to-please
therapist said that she had been taught to close the 'escape

hatches' as a matter of course with all of her clients. Steiner, still amazed, said, 'When I talked about getting clients to agree to not committing suicide I was working in a mental hospital with crazy people. For God's sake don't put ideas into the heads of well-functioning clients!'

Of the 'myths' that continue to linger in the background of humanistic and integrative therapies is the myth that can be traced back to Rogers (1951) and his 'Core Conditions' of empathy, congruence, and unconditional positive regard. Even though Rogers himself said that of the three congruence – or the therapist's ability to process and share the way she is being impacted by the client and the client's story – was the most important, there remains an assumption that I meet over and over again when I supervise trainees that therapists must have positive *feelings* towards, as well as positive *regard* for, their clients. I can remember the expression on the face of a newly-qualified therapist when I told her that I found the client she was presenting very hard to like. The therapist looked both relieved and anxious and said, 'I didn't know we were allowed not to like our clients.' In hindsight this was a moment of transformation for the therapist, who has gone from strength to strength since allowing herself to feel and think in ways that might shock the earnest beginner. She has come to trust that it is often in her more unsavoury responses to a client that the sources of the client's injuries are discovered and through which the therapist's ability to feel empathy for and hold the client emerges.

Another 'myth' in the humanistic world is that of mutuality and horizontality. In my experience true mutuality is not possible in any relationship where one party has ultimate responsibility for another. When that is so it is not possible to give the experience of each party 'equal' weight. The therapist needs to attend to her experience in the room, moment by moment, but also needs to 'bracket' all sorts of thoughts and feelings and impulses. The client has no obligation to do this. In fact we actively encourage our clients to bring us their deepest thoughts and feelings. We also insist on some level that they control their impulses when in the room with us. It would not, for example, be acceptable for a client to hit their therapist. In most settings these days it is not acceptable to smoke.

Furthermore with the 'professionalization' of psychotherapy and counselling, and the accompanying codes of ethics and practice, our clients have power over us that we do not have over them. They can – and more and more frequently do – take out complaints that are not based on gross professional misconduct, like sexual or financial impropriety, but rather on perceived misattunement and ordinary, human frailty that can neither be proven by the client nor defended by the therapist because of a commitment to confidentiality that extends beyond the termination of even an unsuccessful therapeutic relationship.

Humanistic psychotherapy's failure to address the power dynamics in the therapeutic relationship goes hand in hand with its philosophical refusal to accept 'dysfunction'. Rowan (2001) describes the humanistic view of the client as being like a plant that, given the right conditions, will thrive. I don't entirely disagree. But I have had the experience of tending plants, giving them sunlight and water and food, only to watch them wither from a 'disease' that has taken hold at the roots. I believe that an effective psychotherapist needs to be skilled at offering relational conditions *and* needs also to have a healthy respect for what is not in his or the client's awareness or even control. This process gets played out in unconscious

9

or non-verbal communication between therapist and client.

To be or not to be?

Current research indicates that relationship factors are curative. This does not mean – as it is sometimes misinterpreted – that just *being* with another person with the intention to be empathic, congruent, and to respect them unconditionally is enough. I believe that the followers of Rogers and other more humanistic or 'third force' theorists have caused the pendulum to swing too far away from *doing* towards simply *being*. As a supervisor I find that single school approach trainees tend to become evangelical about *being*. This zeal often leads to what one of my supervisors used to call 'gratuitous self-disclosure' of the therapist's experience, to the point where the client can become lost in the trainee therapist's enthusiasm about his newly discovered ability to report what's going on for him.

I don't want to appear to knock a therapist's attempt to know himself better in the clinical encounter, as I believe that it is essential to learn to know oneself in relationship through the psychotherapy that accompanies and, ideally, continues after the training. There is also no doubt in my mind that 'people' people are better therapists than academics or technicians. But I want to make the point that *both* people skills *and* technical knowledge and skills must support each other in the therapy. Technique, which needs always to be supported by theory or collective wisdom, must not get in the way of what's happening in the room *and* what's happening in the room must inform technique.

Countertransference issues for supervision

One of the assumptions that informs my work as a therapist and as a supervisor is that being able to 'read' and process transference – or the client's mostly non-verbal communication of archaic experience – is essential to a successful therapeutic outcome. I feel dismayed when I meet humanistic therapists who tell me that they don't work with the transference. This is nonsense. All therapists work with transference. It is in the field of any relationship, particularly ones in which there is a power differential. Humanistic therapists work with the transference differently from more psycho-dynamically trained therapists in that they name and observe it rather than primarily interpret it.

In all areas of life people very quickly get into transferential relationships with one another. Check your reactions the next time you see flashing lights in your rearview mirror, or are questioned by a customs or immigration official, or when a colleague junior to you makes a mistake or gets a promotion, and you'll see what I mean.

I believe that the key ingredient in psychotherapy is the therapist's ability to recognize, manage, and work with her countertransference responses or, in plain language, with all the emotional and somatic responses that a therapist has towards a client. As a supervisor of trainee or newly qualified therapists, I have noticed that it is often a challenge to get them to bring their 'negative' responses to their clients into supervision. I give an example in the next chapter of enacting my terror and dread of a particularly challenging client by failing to hear the doorbell ring. I was in training at the time and did not feel able to bring my feelings to supervision because I feared being seen as not up to it. (The client had been referred to me by my supervisor who had previously been my therapist.) I was frightened in supervision and frightened in the consulting room, and enacted this in a way that increased my client's expectation of being abandoned as well as her sense of entitlement. We worked through it. I was fortunate.

In order for countertransference to be a reliable source of information about the therapeutic journey the trainee therapist must take his own therapy seriously and be able to enter into it as unfettered as possible by external forces. When I was a trainee there was only a handful of qualified therapists to choose from, as it was a requirement of the training that I work with a more senior member of my training institute. That meant that my therapist was also my supervisor and trainer for at least some of the time. In hindsight I realize that, as much as I thought I took my therapy seriously, there were aspects of myself that I kept hidden. Fortunately, as there are more qualified psychotherapists available to be therapists for trainees, there is less of what I have come to refer to as a 'transferential web'. Nevertheless, relationships – both current and past – do impact the therapeutic relationship when the client is a trainee, and need to be considered for their influence on the supervisory relationship as well.

The transferential web

Figure 1 uses Lewin's (1952)concept of 'field' to illustrate the forces in the supervisory relationship when the supervisee is a trainee. It can also be applied to the therapeutic

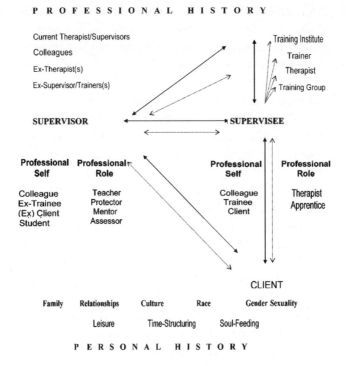

PROFESSIONAL HISTORY

Current Therapist/Supervisors
Colleagues
Ex-Therapist(s)
Ex-Supervisor/Trainers(s)

Training Institute
Trainer
Therapist
Training Group

SUPERVISOR ⟷ **SUPERVISEE**

| Professional Self | Professional Role | | Professional Self | Professional Role |

Colleague
Ex-Trainee
(Ex) Client
Student

Teacher
Protector
Mentor
Assessor

Colleague
Trainee
Client

Therapist
Apprentice

CLIENT

| Family | Relationships | Culture | Race | Gender Sexuality |

Leisure   Time-Structuring   Soul-Feeding

PERSONAL HISTORY

Figure 1. The supervision field *or* the transferential web.

relationship when the client is a trainee, or a member of the psychotherapist's institute or training organization.

Both supervisor and supervisee bring their personal as well as professional history to the relationship. I am particularly interested in the 'professional history', which includes for supervisees their training institute, their trainer(s) and training group and, of course, their therapist. The supervisor's 'professional history' includes her past and current supervisors and therapists as well as the colleagues with whom she trained, who may now be friends, lovers, fellow committee/staff members, or rivals.

13

It is likely that there will be some overlap between the cast of characters in the supervisor's professional past and the supervisee's current professional and collegial relationships. I believe that it is essential for any successful supervisory or therapeutic relationship with a trainee or a colleague to make 'the transferential web' overt. I inquire as a matter of course about the other professionals in the trainee client or supervisee's field. I want to be as careful as I can not to put myself unwittingly in situations external to the supervisory (or therapeutic) relationship where my 'wearing a different hat' could aversely affect that relationship. For example, I don't want to discover well into the relationship that I have been supervising a client's supervisor. I also need to be careful in a peer supervision group that I do not discuss difficulties that I may be having with a supervisee without realizing that the supervisee may be in therapy with one of my colleagues. As a participant at supervisors' meetings where trainees and their progress are discussed, I need to withdraw if one of those trainees is my client. I may also need to get support in my own therapy and supervision to manage what may be evoked in me when a supervisee brings difficulties with a fellow trainee (who may be a client) or with the trainer (who may be a former trainer, therapist, supervisor, supervisee, or client of mine). You see how it can get complicated?

The supervisor and supervisee each have a formal contract (represented in Figure 1 by the solid lines) with the training institute concerning supervision, even if it is unwritten. The supervisee agrees to attend fortnightly supervision and the supervisor agrees, for example, to write bi-annual reports. What can, on the surface, seem relatively straightforward, has the potential for complication when the supervisee brings dynamics of competition, idealization, and regression from his professional history (represented in the figure by the dotted lines) into the supervisory relationship. The supervisor is often, unwittingly, set up to 'fight' with the trainer. I remember trying to help a trainee to see how his client was projecting her father on to him and being told that, according to the supervisee's trainer, there *is* no such thing as projection. In my experience it is left to the supervisor to deconstruct the dogma that trainees introject from their side of the professional field or, at least, to help them to see that there is more than one way to look at relational phenomena.

The terms 'personal' and 'professional', as I have used them in Figure 1, describe and inform the many selves that meet in the supervisory relationship. As a supervisor I emphasize mutuality in the supervisory relationship. Having said that, however collegial I may want to feel with my supervisee, I need to remember that there may be times when I need, metaphorically, to grab him by the seat of his pants to keep him from running into traffic. I also try to remember that I was once in the supervisee's shoes and found it uncomfortable.

The supervisory relationship operates at different levels from moment to moment. I can – and must – identify with my supervisee from my past experience. At the same time, in the effective present I need also to be teacher, mentor, protector (of the supervisee and the client), and assessor, while simultaneously modelling good practice and methods of intervention.

Guidelines for supervisors

I will offer you here a version of the model of supervision that I have developed and written of earlier with my colleague and partner, Penny Daintry (Kearns & Daintry, 2000).

Teach beginning supervisees about supervision

When I was a trainee, the standard approach to supervision was to ask the supervisee what she wanted from each session. I used to hate this and felt put on the spot and exposed. One of our colleagues makes the analogy that asking a beginning supervisee what she wants from supervision is like a waiter asking someone to place his order when he has no idea what is on the menu. The diner might choose the safe option of steak, because it is familiar, and be deprived through lack of information of a more varied and satisfying meal. Trainees often have very little input on their course as to the nature of supervision. Even when they do, part of establishing a successful supervisory relationship needs to include some discussion of what is and what is not on offer.

Supervisors of beginning therapists need to be aware of the impossibility of teaching into an abstraction. It will not be possible for beginners to assimilate information about interpersonal processes of which they have no experience. It's a bit like reading about the history and customs of a place before you visit it. It will make much more sense on the plane on the way home.

Convey a belief that mistakes are normal and that 'feedback' is a necessary part of the process; model self-assessment

Acknowledging that becoming a competent, ethical and compassionate psychotherapist is a life-long process gives an inclusive edge to a new working relationship because it brings the supervisor and supervisee together on a shared road. Helping supervisees to have realistic expectations of themselves is vital, and I tend to talk about my experience as a trainee in order to normalize what they are going through. I try to get across to my supervisee the message that their inner critic and the high expectations they have of themselves may far exceed what I expect from them. I remember a supervisor of mine who used to say, 'Relax. This isn't brain surgery. They'll live.'

I hope, also, to communicate my belief that psycho-therapists must find in themselves the ability to live with *not* knowing, and to acknowledge that this can be a painful process, particularly for those who defend against feelings of inadequacy by relying on things they have learnt.

When a supervisee gets something wrong, try to give feedback by explaining how to do this better next time, and by describing this as their 'growing edge' rather than as a mistake. A dialogic way of beginning to give some potentially difficult feedback might be to generalize and to say, 'Beginning therapists often find it difficult to . . .'.

If a supervisee's sense of self is very fragile he may need to perceive the supervisor as 'perfect' until he is more internally supported to tolerate difference. With supervisees who are reasonably robust, I try to normalize mistakes by sharing my own, and to model self-assessment by regularly assessing *my* performance through using examples from my work with clients. If you don't feel comfortable with this level of self-disclosure, try giving more general examples, prefaced by 'I have a colleague who . . .'

Name and expect competition

This is particularly important in supervision groups. One member of a supervision group of four was having great difficulty with what she perceived as strengths in the others that she did not possess. She disempowered herself in the supervision sessions to such an extent that, on one occasion, without an intervention from anyone, she criticized herself and her work so harshly that she reduced herself to tears. When the supervisor gently helped her to differentiate what she was projecting on to the others from how she was actually working with her client, the group started to unscramble their myths of the 'perfect' therapist and each member – including the supervisor – was eventually able to acknowledge her desire to be the 'best'. Competition then became something that could be lived with and even enjoyed.

Identify, name, and fight transference

When supervising beginning therapists the supervisor can feel invited into a quasi-therapeutic relationship. I know that this has happened when I find myself feeling uncharacteristically withholding, controlling, or over-protective, or when my supervisees continue to bring their difficulties with another colleague to me. The boundary between therapy and supervision is a delicate one and will, inevitably, be crossed from time to time. When this happens it can be helpful to name any transference phenomena ('I'm not your mother, therapist, etc.'), to make overt any reparative goals and to get the supervision back on track as soon as possible.

Get into the habit of recommending your supervisee to work on their relational 'growing edges' in therapy

As the main aim of supervision is to attend to the client–therapist relationship, when interruptions in the supervisor–supervisee relationship become figural and cannot be worked through usefully as parallel process, I prefer the supervisee to take their 'transferential' issues to therapy. If they cannot be resolved, I consider the option of referring the supervisee to a colleague for supervision in order to avoid a protracted focus on healing the past in the present at the expense of the client work.

It needs to be said that there will always be some trainees who resent the requirement for personal therapy as part of their training and who meet the requirement by 'attending' rather than engaging in their therapy sessions. When this is the case the supervisor is faced with a dilemma, because a supervisee who is not able to engage in therapy is also going to be unable to manage his counter-transference usefully. The trainee's blind spots or no-go areas can often get played out in supervision. For example, a supervisee who is afraid of her anger is likely to lodge that anger somewhere else. The supervisor is just as suscept-ible to projective identification (see Chapter Two) as any therapist and may feel powerfully pulled to enact with the supervisee that which the supervisee is unable to face in himself. I tell my supervisees at the start of our relationship that things will emerge in their relationships with their clients that may become obvious through a parallel process in our relationship and that I will expect them to work on this in therapy and to discuss their insights as they relate to their development as therapists in supervision.

Keep a sense of humour

Louise, my first supervisor, was a Freudian. She was also incredibly encouraging through her use of humour and her well-timed ability to tell stories on herself. Once I was having a difficult time with a client and agonised for days whether or not to tell Louise that I was gay. I finally screwed up the courage and spilt the beans. Louise's response to my revelation was, 'You think you've got trouble. I'm a triplet.' Another time when I said that I had been pretty useless all week because I was distracted by something that was going on in my life she said, 'Not to worry. Sometimes they just need someone to watch the movie with them.' I often find that it is through humour and a sense of the absurd that I can reach a healing place in a supervisee who takes himself too seriously.

Make time for relationship maintenance

I allow time for 'relationship maintenance' in individual or group supervision in order to attend to what is happening in the room, and what might be impacting us from outside the room and, therefore, to increase the potential for collaboration rather than projection and regression.

Name and expect shame

I see shame as just one of many potential events in the supervisory field that are to be expected and can be worked with. Having said that, the dynamics of the supervisory relationship make shame a potentially disabling force in the field that will only intensify if it is avoided (see Chapter Seven).

Take all 'reviews' seriously

In another life I used to manage dance companies. One of my mentors when I was in my twenties was a choreographer who, when interviewed and asked how she dealt with critics, answered, 'If I'm going to believe the good reviews I need to believe the bad ones too.' It is very tempting to infantilize and pathologize trainees when they tell us things that are difficult to hear or that don't fit with our view of ourselves. Fight the pull to do this as much as is possible. And remember that trainees *will* believe that you have the all the answers and may even see you as more 'evolved' than they are. They may need to hold on to their view of the supervisor as 'sorcerer' but the supervisor must diligently fight the urge to agree with them. Apart from the likelihood of becoming lost in a hall of mirrors, attending to only our positive reviews breeds therapists who can allow neither a client's less than positive feelings nor their own to inform the therapy.

Note

1.   I do not separate these two ways of responding and agree with Racker (1968) and others that counter-transference is all of the responses that the therapist has to the client.

CHAPTER TWO

FRAGILE SELF-PROCESS

In the previous chapter we looked at some of the challenges for supervisors of trainee psychotherapists, including how to support supervisees to be available to 'use' themselves in a clinical relationship. The focus of that chapter was on the influences in the 'field' – including myth and transference – that the supervisor needs to understand in order to help the trainee to be a more effective practitioner

We also looked at the relationship between *being* vs. *doing*, arriving at the place where both the person of the therapist *and* technique were partners in the work. In this chapter I want to highlight the existential, intrapsychic, and interpersonal dynamics of the therapeutic relationship. Over the last few years I've made a sort of 'map' for myself and my supervisees that seeks to divide people into categories in order to emphasize the commonality of human experience as well as to underscore that we feel and think and behave with some people differently than we feel and think and behave with others. When this happens in a therapeutic relationship, I believe that we need to enter fully into those thoughts and feelings in an internal dialogue and in supervision in order to see them as something the client is telling us that he has not got the words to say. Those dialogues, then, inform how we are and what we do in the clinical encounter.

It is unpopular in humanistic circles to say that we're *doing* something to people. Humanistic therapists don't 'treat patients' we 'work with clients'. Sometimes I think we forget that people are paying us because they don't feel 'well' and they want to 'get better' and that we've spent a lot of time and money learning to help them to do that. This inevitably involves a certain amount of technical relating that goes beyond human relating. Whatever our philosophical and theoretical orientation, we need to know more explicitly about the 'why' of clinical relating in order to be more effective therapists, on the one hand, and not to do harm on the other. I hope we can agree that there are some things you would do with some clients and not others, just as there are ways that you might be with some that would be unhelpful with others. Trainees need help in order to be able to differentiate between the kind of client you can be more 'yourself' with and those you can't.

The internal 'map' I create from my experience as a client, my clinical experience, and my knowledge of theory, gives me some way of explaining to myself what I am doing and thinking and feeling and why, even if I discard it the next day. Maps are useful to get from one place to another but not all maps work with all methods of transport. I live in Chiswick and know the surrounding area well. Even so, when I want to walk to Richmond along the river – a walk I've done many times – I'll use a different 'internal' map from the ones I would use to travel there by tube or by car. When I go walking in a place I don't know well, factors such as the degrees of familiarity and of risk in the journey and the time I've got to do it in dictate to a greater or lesser degree the need to use somebody else's map.

I see my part of my responsibility as a supervisor to be lending my map to my supervisees until they have developed their own internal representation of the therapeutic journey. I've had a go at putting my 'internal' diagnostic map on paper. Figure 2 is my attempt to hold what can seem contradictory diagnostic models at the same time as discerning and, to a certain extent, categorizing my more characteristic responses to certain kinds of people. You may share some of my responses and will, of course, have your own.

My map is an attempt to integrate theoretical knowledge from gestalt, object relations, the *DSM* and, at the same time, to manage and to understand what is being evoked in me by the client. Central to it are the three object relations categories of 'schizoid', 'borderline', and 'narcissistic', around which I have grouped 'personality disorder' categories from the *DSM*, held in a framework that includes the fundamental 'existential' issues that are central to the meaning the client makes of the world, their primary interpersonal contact style, and the response that is evoked in the therapist.

Before I continue to talk you through the map, I want to flag up two further assumptions that inform my thinking about 'fragile self-process'. I take it for granted that the terms 'schizoid', 'borderline', and 'narcissistic' apply to each of us. When I refer to 'the client', I am also taking for granted that both supervisee and supervisor are or have been 'the client' to other therapists and supervisors. We couldn't possibly understand some of the stranger ways people experience life and relate to others if we didn't have those parts ourselves. This assumption underscores my belief that effective psychotherapists need to accept and get to know their fragile parts, otherwise what is not known and 'humanized' will undermine the work or, at the very least, make it more difficult for the therapist. When I was

Central Issues	***Safety***		***Trust***	***Abandonment/ Engulfment***		***Worth***	***Status***
Object Relations		Schizoid		Borderline			Narcissistic
Defences		***Master/Slave***		***Clinging/Distancing***			***Idealising/Devaluing***
DSM		Schizotypal Paranoid Schizoid	Avoidant	Borderline Dependent	Histrionic Passive/Aggressive		Narcissistic Obsessive/Compulsive (Paranoid)
Sub Groups	Withdrawn Schizoid	Secret Schizoid	Quiet Borderline	PTSD Borderline	In-your-face Borderline	Closet Narcissist	Exhibitionistic Narcissist
Countertransference							
	Impatience (responsibility) Feeling controlled Boredom Sleepiness Anxiety		*Over-Protectiveness Idealising Deadening*	*Caretaking (responsibility) Feeling invaded Feeling like a terrible person Irritation/Rage*		*Terror Confusion Hate Dread*	*Envy Guilt Feeling redundant Inadequacy Feeling incompetent Glowing*

Figure 2. Fragile self-process – a working map.

in training, 'borderline' was just another word for 'hell on wheels'. Consequently it was a long time before I was able to recognize and get to know the borderline parts of me. (No doubt these were perfectly obvious to others.) Interestingly, I had a reputation for working well with borderlines. The simple explanation is that something in me understood something in them. Another, less simple, explanation is that what was not in my conscious awareness *activated* the borderline aspects in these clients.

This second explanation sits well with the postmodern view that 'self' is a construct and is inherently relational. If 'self' is a process or verb rather than a noun, then self-process *is* essentially fragile. This is my second assumption. Once we no longer think of 'self' as a private, observable, knowable place – although certain aspects of self *are* consistent and predictable – 'self' as a process in relationship with others and the environment is equally unpredictable and dependent on an ability to negotiate the unexpected. If you're the kind of person who has a reasonably positive and consistent history of the experience of 'other' – including your body – even when 'other' doesn't always behave the same way, you'll be better prepared to deal with and to expect the unexpected than someone who had a reasonably traumatic and inconsistent history of internal and external relationships. It follows, then, that the more inconsistent the history of relationships the more fragile the self-process.

Existential issues

Various writers (Greenberg, 1989; Manfield, 1992; Masterson, 1976; Masterson & Klein, 1995) identify what

27

I would call existential issues that are central and defining for each of the three 'self-process' categories: safety and trust for the schizoid, abandonment and engulfment for the borderline, and status for the narcissist. I have placed these on a continuum on the top line of Figure 2, moving 'trust' to a point between 'schizoid' and 'borderline' and adding 'worth' between 'borderline' and 'narcissistic' in order to describe certain less obvious types of schizoid and narcissistic experience of self in relationship.

Defences?

The ways that each of us develop to anticipate and to manage what is predictably negative and the unexpected in all its guises are called different things in different therapeutic languages: resistances, defences, interruptions to contact, rackets. As a supervisor, I want to convey that I regard these phenomena as sources of learning for the therapist and as a fight for health on the client's part. Whatever the theories say about what supports this in the psyche, or soul, or orbito-frontal cortex, I make another basic assumption, which is that clients – particularly those who are 'stuck' or consistently unresponsive, even attack-ing – are trying to show us what's wrong so that we can fix it. This is easy for me to forget when on the receiving end of a client's rage.

Most of us can readily identify the characteristics of the stereotypes in each of the three categories: the schizoid who is cut off from his emotions and his body, who prefers his own company – or that of his computer – to the company of others; the borderline who, like a toddler, needs holding and containing and who will push you to the limits of your tolerance through pyrotechnical displays of emotion and desperate attempts to get looked after; the narcissist, who is so busy polishing his own mirror that he experiences the light from the mirror you hold up as an irritating, distracting glare.

Very few of the clients I have met, either as a clinician or as a supervisor, fit the stereotypes. More often than not the diagnosis, or 'working hypothesis', is drawn from a combination of factors, including *how* the person is in relationship and how that impacts the therapist. The second line of Figure 2 names the primary ways of relating to the world employed by clients who fall into each of the three categories.

People with a schizoid self-process are in a sort of self-imposed emotional exile. I think of them as having parts that are frozen in time. They are either terrified or seriously distrusting of intimacy, and tend to have relationships through fantasy or with inanimate objects or animals. They can seem to lead their lives under a banner that reads: 'control or be controlled'. Often what relationships they do have take on the flavour of 'master–slave' units (Masterson & Klein, 1995), and the therapeutic relationship is no exception.

The borderline dance is characterized by clinging and distancing defences (Manfield, 1992). Sometimes this is subtle and is disguised as compliance; with other clients it can be a bit like a roller-coaster ride. 'Clinging–distancing' is different from 'master–slave' in that the latter is about keeping one's distance through control and the former is supported by attempts of one kind or another not to be – or to stay – separate. Fear of 'abandonment' is the apparent central issue of people with a borderline self-process, which co-exists with and may conceal an equally powerful yet often less apparent struggle in response to 'engulfment' that is also central to the borderline experience of living between no containment on the one hand and too much containment on the other.

More narcissistically challenged people tend to be grandiose in ways that are not always immediately apparent, and devaluing of others and, in the case of the 'closet narcissist' of themselves. This process of inflation and deflation can challenge even an experienced therapist's capacity to offer the empathy that people like this need in order to begin the slow process of healing.

DSM categories or the reason for labels

Having said earlier that each of us has aspects of fragile self-process that can range from a personality 'style' to a full-blown 'disorder' I want to say something about how I use the term. What I mean by fragile self-process is that in certain important relationships or under stressful conditions we fall back into more infantile ways of being in the world and rely on more 'primitive' defences such as splitting, idealization, and devaluation and projective identification in desperate attempts to make ourselves heard. However, these defences interfere with rather than enhance functioning. We may act impulsively rather than observing our experience, differentiating between the past and the present and acting in our own best, adult interest. We really are our own worst enemy and need to discover the ability to forgive ourselves and to laugh lovingly at our attempts to learn to live within limits.

Trainee therapists who believe that the goal of therapy is to help their clients to feel, or to 'lose their minds and come to their senses', are asking for trouble if they meet a client whose ability to control their emotions and associated behaviour is impaired. Some of us need to feel less or to tolerate what we do feel as opposed to expressing ourselves cathartically. Others need to be gently and carefully un-frozen and not bombarded with statements about how the therapist is feeling or with questions about our own feelings. As a friend of mine says, when he first entered therapy he wouldn't have known a feeling if he fell over one. I can remember being both fascinated and terrified by the displays of all kinds of feeling in the first therapy group I joined when I started my TA training. My fascination won in the end, because if I had stayed with my terror I could easily have run screaming from the building.

The reason we talk about 'transference' and its primary mechanisms, projection and splitting, is that the degree of a client's fragility is related to their ability to see the therapist as a reasonably benign entity who has experience in helping people and who intends to help them. Clients with a more fragile self-process tend to have difficulty relating to the therapist as a separate person. Or, through splitting, they relate to the therapist as two completely different people, or blow up one aspect of the therapist as though it was their entirety.

These clients tend, one way or another, to talk about other people or to focus on other things more than on themselves. They can also very quickly make the therapist, who they may have known for no more than five minutes, central in their outer world and inner drama. I remember a new client who came into the room, sat down, looked me straight in the eye and said, 'I know you'd rather be doing almost anything else on this beautiful day than

31

sitting here with me but I'm paying you so you can just shut up and listen.' I felt like turning my head to look over my shoulder to see who she was really talking to until I remembered that it was just the two of us. I didn't know then the things that I know now that can support me just to sit still long enough to let my body and emotions help me to know how to respond. Without some diagnostic model the therapist can feel as if they are drowning in the transference. Theory, or the collective experience of those who went before me, helps me to stay afloat.

Manfield (1992), who trained at the Masterson Institute, has grouped the categories of personality 'disorder' from the *DSM III-R* around the three object relations headings. I find this way of organizing these types of people more useful than the *DSM* 'Cluster' system.[1] Manfield puts the 'schizotypal', 'schizoid', and 'avoidant' personalities under the heading of schizoid object relations. I have moved the avoidant label to a point on the continuum between 'schizoid' and 'borderline' as, in my experience, 'avoidant' clients often have a foot in both camps. I also include the 'paranoid' diagnostic label under 'schizoid' as well as 'narcissistic' as, in my experience, predominately paranoid features exist in both object relations categories, yet the central issue differs in that clients with a schizoid structure have a paranoia that is supported by their fundamental sense of being unsafe in the world whereas narcissistic paranoia tends to put the emphasis on the self in danger as opposed to others being dangerous. The schizoid who is paranoid says, '*people* are out to get me' with the emphasis on 'people'; the paranoid narcissist says 'people are out to get *me*'. I agree with Manfield that the *DSM* 'borderline' and 'dependent' belong under borderline object relations, the 'dependent' personality type employing mostly clinging defences in a desperate attempt to get taken care of, and that the 'histrionic' and 'passive–aggressive'[2] personality types share features of both borderline and narcissistic object relations, each employing clinging defences to get you to look after them but also lashing out with devaluing and critical defences if you – and believe me you will – get it wrong. These are the sort of clients who are most likely to take out complaints against authority figures who fail them. As Benjamin (1993) says of her experience of working with passive–aggressive clients 'I could give you examples but I'm afraid to.' Finally, Manfield places people who meet the *DSM* criteria for the diagnosis of 'narcissistic', 'obsessive–compulsive' and 'paranoid' personality disorders under the narcissistic heading.

Sub-groups

Figure 2 divides the object relations categories into subgroups that roughly correspond with the *DSM* categories on the line above. At the beginning of the continuum I have put what I call the 'frozen schizoid'. This is the more classic schizoid presentation of a client who is very much 'in his head', emotionally 'dead', and relationally distant. This is followed by what Klein – Ralph, not Melanie – refers to as the 'secret schizoid' (Masterson & Klein, 1995). This corresponds with the *DSM* 'avoidant' category and describes the more socialized schizoid who appears to function well in the world, has many friends but few confidantes, and is seemingly competent and successful but is secretly suffering, isolated from others by a fear of intimacy. For these clients to be close to someone means to risk being appropriated which, in their minds, means being controlled by another and ultimately humiliated. Unlike the 'frozen schizoid' these clients often have access to anger, either when alone or in public places, but are rarely able to express their anger with those in their inner circle and that includes the therapist. While on the surface friendly, they may, though, be prickly and sensitive to rejection. Yet, when offered empathy, unlike the narcissists among us, who find it soothing, they are likely to react as though further wounded or to regress to a point of earlier wounding (see Chapter Three, 'Annalise and the big, ugly bug').

They also use arrogance as a defence but, unlike the narcissist who is arrogant because he believes he is better than others who should know this, 'secret schizoids' are arrogant in order to keep their distance from others. These are often very committed clients. They come regularly, appear to work hard and often get absolutely nowhere because, as Fairbairn (1952) pointed out, they play roles in public and privately retreat into fantasy in order to avoid the pain of real emotional contact. These clients will often report feeling as if they come from another planet, or will in other ways describe feeling different to everyone else.

There is overlap here with what Sherwood and Cohen (1994) call the 'quiet borderline'. This is what Deutsch (1942) referred to as the 'as-if' personality, and differs from the 'secret schizoid' in that the underlying defensive dance is not that of master–slave but one of clinging and distancing with the clinging bit well hidden. Unlike the 'secret schizoid', these clients find it very difficult to be alone because they have no inner world or fantasy life in which to seek comfort. They are chameleon-like, their way of being in the world depending on where they are and who they're with. This is not, though, the defensive role-playing of the 'secret schizoid'. These clients have no inner life. They are totally dependent on the therapist for signals about how to be (this is the clinging) *but* they don't talk about their emotional experience in therapy because they haven't got any and, thus, seem a little unreal or too good to be true (and here is the distancing).

'Quiet' borderlines are very difficult to diagnose and to treat because their lack of access to an inner life makes them unaware that they are being anything but genuine and, as a result, are not really able to communicate their distress in therapy other than by making the therapist feel a bit puzzled by her lack of emotional resonance (see Countertransference, below).

Other types of borderline clients – 'PTSD borderlines' and what I call 'in-your-face-borderlines' – are anything but quiet and have a powerful effect on the therapist, but the aetiology of each type is, in my mind, different. PTSD borderlines were children who grew up in chaotic homes where there was alcohol or drug abuse and usually regular physical or sexual abuse. This dreadful start to life is usually compounded in adolescence and adulthood by associating with chaotic and abusive people and partners. Their way of being in the world is typical of the *DSM* borderline personality disorder and usually includes unstable and intense or co-dependent personal relationships (including with the therapist from day one), poor impulse control (sex, drugs, shopping – you name it), self-harm (risk taking, cutting), and mood swings.

Therapy with clients like this is never dull. The chaos in their inner world is brought into the therapy one way or another. These clients know no boundaries – one once rang my doorbell at three in the morning to see if she could have a chat – and the therapist will very quickly in their minds become a possible saviour as well as a potential abuser. This split will get played out in the therapy, with the therapist one minute being someone the client desperately needs (like at three in the morning) and the next being the most terrible of people (because it *is* three in the morning and you mind rather).

As tempting as it may be to not hold firm boundaries with borderline clients, don't do it. Think of them as toddlers who need containing before they can be soothed. Many years ago I saw a young gay man who was a motorcycle messenger. He very quickly developed what I described as 'projectile weeping' in response to the session coming to an end. The closer it got to time being up the more determinedly he would weep. When time was up I picked up his helmet and jacket and ushered him out the door, reminding him of the time of our next appointment. He would sit on the kerb in full view of my front door and anyone else who was around, lean his head on his motorbike and continue to weep. Luckily, I took my lunch break in the slot after his and I didn't have another client coming. I felt like the biggest heel alive and would often have to go to the back of the house and put on music to distract me from my desire to go out and bring him back in until he calmed down. After five weeks of the same pattern I felt at my wits' end. He arrived for his session in week six and said, 'I want to thank you for that.' When I asked him what he was thanking me for he said, 'For not giving in.' I used to be reminded of that client when my partner's grandson would scream blue murder when put in a high chair. After a few minutes he would settle down and seemed genuinely pleased to be in a place where he felt contained and safe.

'In-your-face borderlines', in contrast, had too much containing as infants in that, according to Masterson (1976), they were not encouraged as toddlers to be independent and to explore the world. When they did this, rather than have their experience and emotional reactions accepted and validated, mother would either withdraw as a punishment for their attempts to be separate or would become over-protective and intrusive. For adults, life becomes an often not so subtle battle between the part that wants to grow up and take risks and explore the world and the part that feels often crippling anxiety when faced with a new challenge, because of the fear of inviting the wrath or smothering of the internalized mother. These clients, who are often staggeringly demanding, are closer to the *DSM* dependent personality disorder in that they have difficulty making everyday decisions, require an excessive amount of reassurance from others, go to often humiliating lengths to get looked after (like the messenger above) and are so afraid of being alone and having to look after themselves that they move very quickly from one relationship to another. In their desperate quest to be looked after they usually get rejected and, as much as they cling to the therapist for support, they expect the therapist to reject them just like everyone else eventually does. They also work very hard to get the therapist to do just that.

Where this gets risky for the therapist as opposed to just tedious is if the client has also experienced painful and abrupt rejection later in life involving a third party (losing daddy to mummy in the Oedipal crisis; losing status to a new baby). These rejections are exhibited in histrionic and/or passive–aggressive features that also make these clients highly dramatic and seductive and/or easily wounded. When the therapist makes mistakes with clients like these she is not easily forgiven and may well end up with a complaint being taken out. These clients have a very young desire to seek revenge for having, in their minds, lost out to someone else. The therapist is particularly vulnerable with these clients when another client turns up early or at the wrong time, if she works at home and there is evidence of a child or a partner, or even if she goes on holiday (the client will fantasize that you've gone with somebody else even if you went walking in the woods by yourself). Boundaries again are critical here, but are much more subtle and, often, impossible to enforce. These challenging clients have not fully developed the narcissistic defences that would allow them to feel superior to you and everyone else and therefore to dismiss a therapist who fails them as useless and obviously incompetent while keeping their sense of entitlement intact. A more narcissistically defended client would be perfectly happy to devalue you and the therapy in the sessions, but couldn't be bothered to seek revenge as that would make you potentially too important.

Not all narcissists are obviously grandiose and superior. Some known as 'closet' or 'inverted' narcissists attach themselves to people or institutions from which they receive reflected glory. The classic examples that spring to mind are the stage mother like Rose in 'Gypsy', who sacrifices everything for her reluctant daughter and shouts from the wings, 'Sing out, Louise', or Cardinal Richlieu, the *éminence grise* who had the power while Louis XIV got the glory. Other, less obvious, types of narcissists get their reflected glory not from others but from imagining themselves to be the worst of the worst as opposed to the best of the best. People like this wear their low self-esteem like a badge of honour and are very reluctant to give it up. They have built their identity around the attention that they believe they get from being 'pathetic' and 'useless' and a 'failure' in much the same way that the 'exhibition-istic narcissist' is dependent on achievement and the praise of others for 'self food'.

Bob Resnick, an American Gestalt therapist, used to say that mental health is being able to do something even though it might make your mother happy. Narcissistic clients are said to be the least successful candidates for psychotherapy because of their preference for self-destruc-tion over experiencing someone else's achievement or because of their need for perfect mirroring.

Countertransference

It would seem that one of the commonalities of human experience is that certain personality types evoke reason-ably consistent countertransference responses. The thera-pist's countertransference is particularly diagnostic when the client is not very verbal or is unclear about what they want from the therapy. Of course, we also have idiosyn-cratic reactions to our clients that are useful indicators of personality style. One of my colleagues gets what she calls 'that buzz in my head' around certain schizoid clients. Another finds herself humming a tune that her mother used to sing to her after assessing clients who turn out to have a borderline self-process.

I am frequently asked about the difference between countertransference and projective identification. As I have said, I use the term countertransference to describe all of the emotional and somatic responses that a therapist has towards a client. Racker (1968) divides countertransference into two types, complementary and concordant. In complementary countertransference the therapist resonates with how the client is feeling in the here and now or with how the client used to feel at some point in the past. The mechanics of this are projection and identification. In other words, the therapist projects her experience on to the client and then identifies with the client's experience. This is the basis of empathy. In concordant countertransference the mechanics are a bit different. The client projects a figure from the past or from their life outside the therapy on to the therapist, who begins to identify – or empathize – with how that person feels or felt. Because both of their processes are non-verbal forms of communication, they by-pass the therapist's intellect and are often out of the client's awareness. They are simply *felt*.

Sometimes the mechanics of projection and identification get magnified to the point where the therapist feels something akin to possession. I once was overcome with a desire to get a new client who had come for an assessment out of the room as soon as I possibly could. I became unable to hear what the client was saying and thought only about how I could get rid of her. I was able to support myself enough to say that I didn't think I would be able to work with her and suggested that we end the session and I refer her to a colleague. She was quiet for a while and then said, 'That's what my mother used to do.' Almost immediately I felt 'myself' again and experienced being deeply moved as she told me how her mother had never wanted to have a baby and had given her away when she was a week old, returning to visit from time to time, and finally deciding to raise the child herself when she was old enough not to need nappies.

With another client who, after several months of therapy had said very little, I experienced one day such all-consuming rage that I had to have an imaginary conversation with my supervisor in my head to contain it. I finally said to my client, 'I'm beginning to wonder if the difficulty you have talking to me is because of the level of feeling in you.' The client looked at me, let out an ear-piercing shriek and said, 'I feel better now.' That was a turning point in the therapy. The client was then able to begin to find words for her feelings.

In the first example I believe that I experienced some of my client's mother's feelings towards her infant; in the second I may have felt rage that was so blocked from my client's awareness that I had to feel it for her. In both instances I felt as though I had been taken over by a force greater than either of us, making it nearly impossible for me think clearly.

Rage is a countertransference reaction that is common with clients of all presentations. As I have come to understand it, rage that comes from my feelings of inadequacy normally indicates a narcissistic self-process, whereas the rage that results from irritation at being intruded on or even persecuted tends to be evidence of a borderline self-process in the client. The sort of rage reaction I can have to a schizoid self-process seems to come from my impatience with myself that I project on to the client as well as from my disbelief that another human being could be so slow to respond.

Countertransference reactions with clients who are on the 'schizoid' end of the continuum include impatience that stems from a need to take responsibility for the client's progress. The therapist may find himself thinking, 'Not much is going on here? I should be doing more. Why does this person keep coming to talk about carriage driving?' The therapist may also feel controlled, bored, sleepy, and anxious. In my experience these responses resonate with the archaic 'hate' that the client is defending against.

With clients who fall between the schizoid/borderline points on the continuum, the therapist may become over-protective in that she finds herself holding back her responses, using the excuse that the client isn't ready yet. This can also be supported by a sort of idealizing of the client, particularly of the 'quiet borderline' presentation. I once worked with a client about whom I found myself thinking, 'Why is she seeing a therapist? Particularly me. She's more sorted than I am.' This woman had it all and I wanted some of it. One day, several years into whatever you would call what we were doing together, she broke down uncontrollably and told me that she'd been having an affair with a derelict drug addict for the past five years, was HIV positive, and her husband had left her with the children to live in another country. With another client, Ruth, to whom I will continue to refer throughout these chapters I often felt nothing. I liked her and I had all sorts of thoughts about her but I felt dead from the neck down. I was able to understand this as resonance with a schizoid core, even though her behaviour might have led me to accept her 'borderline' self-diagnosis (see Chapter Four).

With borderline clients the therapist is likely to be pulled to take care of them and to offer them things that she wouldn't dream of offering other clients. A supervisee recently told me that she has agreed to see a client on a Saturday morning and said, 'And I don't work on Saturday mornings!' Boundary disturbances are common with borderline clients and can lead the therapist to feel invaded unless she sets and holds clear limits. As in the example above, the therapist can also feel like a terrible person when confronted with the client's frantic attempts to get you to look after them or to give in to their demands.

Clients who fall between the borderline and narcissistic points on the continuum often induce powerful feelings in the therapist such as terror, confusion, and hate. The therapist can find herself defending against these feelings by dreading the sessions to the point where she fails to turn up for the appointment or, as I once did, by not hearing the doorbell and leaving the poor client standing on my doorstep, thus stepping straight into her fear of abandonment and her fragile sense of entitlement (see section on Countertransference Issues in Supervision).

A colleague of mine once said, 'You know that feeling you get when you think that this client ought to be seeing a *real* therapist?' Indeed I do. With more obviously narcissistic clients the therapist often feels the feelings of inadequacy that the client actively defends against feeling. I can find myself feeling redundant and/or incompetent. I know my client is narcissistically challenged when I start thinking that I probably ought to have gone to law school. Narcissistic clients who endlessly boast of their own achievements often arouse feelings of envy in me, accompanied by feelings of guilt. I can also feel like a bit of a stage-mother myself, and find myself wanting to boast in supervision that *my* client is a famous actress. Conversely, with more 'closet' narcissists who cloak their feelings of superiority in a shroud of inferiority and failed creativity, the 'agent' in me gets activated and I find myself wanting to 'represent' them in some way to the world and showing how clever *I* am by coming up with 'great' ideas for how they could publish that book, sell those paintings, or market that great-but-unrecognized idea. Usually the last thing I feel instinctively or easily is compassion, and I find that I have to employ technical empathy rather than an empathy that is deeply felt.

To love and to work

When asked how he viewed mental health, Freud is reported to have said (Erikson, 1963) 'to love and to work'. When I assess a new client or meet a new client through a supervisee I am looking for information about the meaning of love and of work in his life so that I can begin to form a picture about where his fragility may lie and how he manages – or defends against – it.

In our society, one of the ways that we show our ability to be separate from our parents and even our partners is through finding work. With any luck the work we choose also gives us an outlet for creative expression. I once went to buy underwear at Macy's in New York. Having made my selection I headed towards the till to find that at least ten other shoppers had beat me to it. I joined the queue muttering to myself that I didn't feel like wasting my precious time in New York waiting in a crowded, airless basement to buy cheap knickers. I was preparing to abandon my quest when I realized that in the time I had been moaning to myself the queue had reduced by half. The woman at the till was remarkable, not just for the speed with which she moved people along but also for her good humour. When I got to the front of the queue I told her as much and she said, 'This could be a really boring job if I wanted it to be. I decided to make it work for me.' She had chosen to alleviate boredom – hers and others' – by making it a matter of personal pride to be fast and to make people laugh.

Each of us has a relationship with and feelings about achievement. Some seek it to gain personal satisfaction and are appropriately anxious about fear of failure. Others obsess about failure to the point where no imperfection is tolerated in self or others. Interestingly, success in people with a borderline self-process *increases* anxiety. This is because to be successful is to be separate and to be separate feels, at an emotional level, like being abandoned. Thus, people with a borderline self-process sabotage success. This is not to say that borderline clients are not successful. Many are, but, because success leads to an expectation of abandonment or engulfment, sabotage in one form or another often quickly follows any new achievement. Sabotage takes many forms, even in supposedly 'high' achievers. The company director, having clinched a big deal earlier in the day, may pick a fight with her partner that evening that will have the effect of not being able to feel good about her success because she'll be too busy being in a bad mood. More dramatic forms of sabotage range from getting so drunk the night before a big event that the event itself is spoiled or missing out on it altogether to crashing the car on the way to an interview. Less than high-achieving borderlines will let their extreme dependence on another or their poor impulse control keep them from ever fulfilling their creative potential by believing that someone else's needs are more important than their own in the first instance or by living life so impulsively that their own (and usually others') inner resources are scarce.

In contrast success makes a narcissist feel excited and important rather than self-loathing and anxious. Schizoid people feel safe with their success since being successful allows them to feel in control. The successful schizoid wants to own the company so that he can make people do things his way; the successful narcissist wants to own the company because of the status she derives from being at the top. Schizoids are often very successful at things they can do on their own, from artistic expression to working with computers. They often don't seek or at least don't require feedback from others because they are getting what they most want from life: a self-sufficiency that protects them from needing others and thus experiencing disappointment and vulnerability. Narcissists, too, may enjoy apparently lone pursuits, but the world, or at least their world, will hear about them and so will you. In short, in work and success the narcissist seeks praise and the schizoid seeks control. Interestingly, borderlines do genuinely seek success for its own sake but will be waylaid by the anxiety that success – and successes in the therapy are no exception – inevitably brings.

In relationship – and this includes the therapeutic relationship as well as 'intimate' relationships – narcissists seek mirrors rather than people. The other is used, although not always deliberately, to reflect aspects of themselves. Without this feedback loop the narcissist can feel anxiety that leads to rage on the one hand and deflation on the other. Schizoids, particularly the 'secret' or avoidant schizoids, often long to be in an intimate relationship but pull back, fearing being exposed and humiliated. Borderlines seek to be taken care of in relationship, even if they appear to be the one who does all the caring. The message is 'I will be everything to you so that you will never leave me'. This is often mistaken by the therapist as a client who 'does good work' in therapy but doesn't shift.

All fragile self-process is characterized by definitions of love that suggest devotion and dependence, dominance and submission, entitlement and long-suffering. Love as other-enriching, unspectacular, and liberating is either unimaginable or remains conceptual and unsustainable. The therapeutic relationship allows for communication at a non-verbal level that can support more 'mature' loving outside the consulting room.

Notes

1. The *DSM III-R* grouped personality disorders into clusters: Cluster A refers to the 'Odd or Eccentric' personality types and includes the schizoid, schizotypal and paranoid; Cluster B personalities – Borderline, Narcissistic, Hystrionic and Anti-Social – are 'Dramatic, Emotional or Erratic' (like Manfield I have excluded the Anti-Social Personality Disorder from my map as I think it describes a kind of person who is not best treated by 'insight-based' or experiential therapies); Cluster C refers to the 'Anxious or Fearful' personality types of Passive–Aggressive, Obsessive–Compulsive, Dependent and Avoidant.
2. The 'Passive–Aggressive' Category does not appear in the *DSM IV*. Interesting, eh?

CHAPTER THREE

SCHIZOID SELF-PROCESS

I include this chapter here because understanding the aetiology and relational dynamics of the schizoid presentation has helped me immeasureably to work more effectively – not just with clients with a schizoid self-process, but also with addictions and eating disorders, which will be the subjects of Chapters Four and Five. I have also come to understand something about the link between schizoid and narcissistic presentation and will share what I have learnt with you.

It was only after fifteen or so years of practice and my own psychotherapy that I had any relational understanding of a schizoid self-process. I eventually realized that a good deal of confusion about the term 'schizoid' comes from the fact that the *DSM* schizoid and the object relations schizoid are not the same thing.[1]

My training included very little input on schizoid self-process. The term was mentioned, particularly by TA writers (Stewart & Joines, 2002; Ware, 1983), who referred to the withdrawn, 'un-feeling' aspects of a schizoid presentation, the goal of therapy being to help these clients to 'get out of their heads' and into their bodies. Just teach them to feel. It all seemed so simple in those days. Over time I have come to realize just how terrifying feeling at all levels is to the more schizoid amongst us.

Laing (1990) described the schizoid experience as having an internal boundary splitting mind and body that precedes the boundary between self and other. It looks something like this:

$$\frac{\text{Self} \mid \text{Other}}{\text{Body}}$$

This self/body split is easy to see in more typically schizoid clients like Nigel. During our first session his stomach rumbled continually and I eventually asked if he was hungry. Nigel looked at his watch, then looked at me and said, 'No.' He was so cut off from his body and his physical sensations that he ate according to the clock and not according to how he was feeling. He described his experience of the world as like 'living behind a wall'. It was, he told me, 'important to keep a safe distance'.

Nigel was an accountant. He was 30 and had never had a sexual relationship. I knew instinctively that it would be a long and delicate journey to introduce him to his body and I had some technical understanding of how to do that. What I didn't have was any theoretical understanding of what would be required of me as a person in a therapeutic relationship that was to last for ten years. I remember thinking about Nigel after our first session and wondering if I would ever reach someone who was so wary of human contact. How, I wondered, do you get to be like that?

How *do* you get to be like that?

Here is what I've come to understand about the development of the schizoid personality style. When an infant cannot get what she wants from the person she needs it from (usually mother) she's got two choices: she can have a tantrum and aggressively express her need or she can –

and this usually follows repeated unsuccessful attempts to get noticed – get more and more needy until need itself seems like the very core of her being. Fairbairn (1941) called this 'love made hungry', and identified the schizoid problem as the terrible fear that one's love has become so devouring that love itself has become destructive.

There is an important distinction between depression, which could be seen as a sort of withdrawal of potentially destructive hate (as in the child who has the tantrum), and the schizoid position, which is the fear of loving lest one's love *or even need of love* should destroy – which is far worse. As Guntrip (1968) says 'the schizoid is hungry for a desirable deserter, the depressive is murderous against a hateful robber' (p. 25). The depressed person turns anger and aggression against himself and feels guilty; the schizoid person withdraws from the intolerable situation of desiring love, believing it to be impossible to have and believing that this impossibility is created by his very need for love itself.

A new client, who was adopted after spending the first six months of her life in what she calls 'a home for babies nobody wanted', brought a dream in which she looked out of the window of her home and saw me standing on the pavement. She wanted me to come in but the grass between the pavement and her front door was long and wet and there was no path. She thought that I might have a lawnmower in the boot of my car but then realized that the house was too messy and ran upstairs to hide. We can imagine that this dream describes the feeling that she has had long before she had the words to give it form, of wanting someone to come into her world yet hopelessly retreating further into it, fearing that her 'mess' would drive them away.

Guntrip points out that schizoid clients show little evidence – or at least awareness – of anger and guilt that might signal depression. The adult who has adapted to life in this way gives an impression – even if it is well buried – of fear and retreat. The lights are on but nobody appears to be at home.

The schizoid client's dilemma is of craving for connection yet not being able to be intimate with or connected to another. He fears destroying and losing the one he desires and being destroyed in turn. So, on the one hand he longs for relationships, but withdraws because relationships are too dangerous to enter into. And he does this, not just for his own protection, but – almost sacrificially – out of a desire to protect and preserve the other.

As Guntrip says, if you believe your hate is destructive you can always find someone else to love while you go on hating (*ibid.*, p. 48). But, if you believe your love is destructive, the situation is terrifying, and it is this terror that is at the core of the schizoid experience of the world. You feel on the one hand impelled into a relationship because of your needs and at the same time driven out again by the fear of exhausting the object of your affection or being devoured by it. This is what Guntrip called the 'in and out programme' (*ibid.*, p. 36).

Johnson (1985) describes the schizoid as the 'hated child.' I'm not so sure that a schizoid self-process always develops from hate. According to Guntrip, hate is 'love grown angry' (1968, p. 36) and implies relationship. Hate always has an object. It is not the opposite of love. The two often go hand-in-hand. The schizoid position is one where indifference in the environment fuels desire, which becomes hunger, and hunger which becomes greed or hunger that has grown anxious about being unsatisfied. The desire is unbearable and is distinguished through being split off.

Schizoid clients fear that everything they have – ideas, fantasies, abilities – will be laid claim to and destroyed by the other. They often grew up in households where nothing could be kept private or where everything became about mother and there was no choice but surrender or retreat. This is the basis of the master–slave dynamic that Masterson and Klein (1995) describe. There can be no private ownership. One exists to serve the master. The price of attachment is enslavement. The alternative is emotional or physical exile.

A client who was the youngest of six children in a working class family talks about growing up in an environment where there was no absence of love but where necessity and economic reality led her to take herself away in order to manage her 'neediness' and to protect the rest of her family. They lived in a two up/two down and she spent most of her free time next door with Mrs Atkinson, a hard-of-hearing old woman who would let her look at her photographs and give her tea. There was no conversation, just a sort of comfort in having some distance from life at home where there was never enough and nothing was private.

Schizoid people are able to cut off most of their intense feelings of fear, hopelessness, and isolation through workaholism, intellectualization, and other distancing defences so that they often do not experience emotional pain (Manfield, 1992). They can appear to be quite successful because of their ability to distance and devote themselves to their work and to make decisions uncluttered by emotions.

The therapeutic relationship

Because the central existential issue for the schizoid is safety and trust he is not going to be inclined to see a therapeutic relationship as safe or as a likely source of comfort or support. He will be selective about what he tells the therapist and may intentionally withhold information. He may genuinely be at a loss to know what is relevant to share with the therapist. This is often experienced clinically as a lack of ability to engage in metaphor or to make links; a refusal to consider that the past is related to the present or that the future could be different from the present. It is more likely to be the case that schizoid clients hold on to their dreams and their memories of the past because they are afraid of the cost of sharing them with anyone – and that includes you. These clients, in my experience, are frozen in time. Their bodies are often rigid; their terror of relationship is often evident in their eyes, which may be glazed and unfocused or on alert.

Some schizoid clients may appear to be sociable and involved with relationships, but are often not fully involved and may be playing a role. Many clients who at first seem to be borderline or narcissistic will reveal a schizoid core over time when a therapeutic alliance has been established. At first the therapist is likely to experience a variety of 'distancing' defences such as intellectualization, detachment, emotional and physical constriction, lack of spontaneity, self-sufficiency, and the need to control. There may also be additional narcissistic defences – particularly arrogance and grandiosity – but if you listen to the music under the words these defences protect a terrified or empty core (Seinfeld, 1991), not a raging or inadequate one. They don't serve, as do a narcissist's defences, to enhance specialness or status, but to maintain a safe-ish distance. The schizoid doesn't avoid people because he feels superior to them; he adopts an attitude of superiority *in order to* avoid them. The borderline fears being abandoned for being separate and feels confused. The schizoid had pre-empted abandonment through a self-imposed exile.

A common countertransference reaction to schizoid clients is that the therapist wonders why they continue coming to therapy. Not only that, these clients are usually always on time and rarely cancel a session. These are the clients who, like Nigel, hide their longing to be found behind an imaginary wall. The more solid the wall the less the therapist will be impacted on an emotional level. My supervisor helped me to understand that a client who appeared to be doing no work at all in therapy and about whom I – unusually – felt absolutely nothing had been so neglected as an infant that she had given up on even the more subtle ways that we can impact each other. She only felt alive when she complained, which she could do 'for England'. I once asked her, after a litany of all the unhelpful people in her life, if I was one of them. She responded without hesitating, 'Oh no. You keep me sane.'

This was news to me. I realized that, on some level, this woman did feel connected to me, but it was far too risky for her to allow herself to be 'seen' by me. Hence the complaining. Schizoid clients have been in a self-imposed exile since infancy and long to be 'found' by the therapists; they may, in fact, *feel* found long before they have any way of letting you know that other than by turning up week after week and boring you rigid.

When I was a trainee on a therapy marathon we were all asked to hide. All but one in the group scrambled

55

around and hid under tables and behind sofas and doors. The therapist asked her why she wasn't hiding. She replied, 'When you really know how to hide you don't need a table.'

Not all schizoids keep away from people – it's not people schizoids are avoiding but intimacy and self-disclosure. Walking constantly the two poles between isolation and engulfment the schizoid compromise is to find what Guntrip calls 'a half-way house position' (1968, p. 61) – neither in nor out. As we saw in the diagnostic map in Chapter Two, the avoidant personality disorder was a new category in the *DSM III-R* that classified what I call the 'socialized schizoid' – the client who longs for relationship but fears being exposed and humiliated. Benjamin (1993) says that people with avoidant aspects to their personalities often get involved in triangular relationships where the risk of true intimacy is less great. Or they become psychotherapists. Think about it. The position of therapist is the ideal 'half-way house position'. We can have intense relationships with our clients knowing that we can call time after fifty minutes and that once the therapy is over it is very unlikely that we will ever see the client – for whom we may have deep feelings of love and respect – again. Is this normal?

How to work?

Because safety and trust are the central relational issues for schizoid people, therapists need to adopt a casual, non-intrusive stance. Anything that smacks of therapeutic technique or interpretation may send the schizoid client packing. This is because they secretly believe that you *can* see inside their heads or that you will try to take them over. In the early days of therapy with schizoid clients I often feel as if we're just hanging out together. Sometime the work will have the flavour of a social chat. The therapist needs to allow this and, in the words of a colleague, to use an oblique angle of relating in order to let trust develop so that the client can risk being seen.

Creating a safe environment is paramount. Hilda was very nervous at our first session and, as luck would have it, there were builders working in the flat next door. I explained the strange noises and saw in her body language that she was still very uncomfortable. I offered to go next door to have a word and she replied that just knowing that I would consider doing that made her feel safer. I learned a lot about schizoid presentation from Hilda, including that these clients often feel easily overwhelmed and need to be in control of some of the intensity of being alone in a small room with another person. After a few weeks of working together I noticed that after about forty minutes Hilda would glaze over. I said, 'You've had enough, haven't you?' and she said, 'Yes. Can I go now?'

I replied that she was free to come and go as she pleased. She did leave, and after that usually stayed for the full fifty minutes but, every once in a while – even after ten years of therapy – she'd say that she had had enough now, was going to leave and she did.

Klein (1995) talks about working with schizoid patients as being like 'pulling teeth' and finally coming to understand that the therapist needs to convey to the client a willingness to wait for her to open up, even if it takes years. And it usually does. Rather than confronting or naming silence as you might with a client with a borderline presentation, Manfield suggests that it is more effective either to

57

wait patiently for the client to communicate or to interpret the schizoid dilemma by saying things like: 'I can imagine that you will need to keep your distance from me until you can be more sure that I'm safe enough to be with'; or 'I wonder if you're worried that if you tell me something about yourself I'll take it away from you and it won't be yours any more'.

The idea is to communicate to the client that you can *understand* how he might feel without *knowing* how he feels, which is something like wanting to but feeling scared to open up.

Interventions that in any way suggest that you know more about the client than the client expects you to know can be very threatening to the working alliance. Empathy needs to be used sparingly and hypothetically. Otherwise the client may feel that you are trying to take her over by defining her emotional experience or will, at the very least, feel intruded upon. It is safer with these clients to gently hypothesize rather than to run the risk of appearing to tell them how they feel or even to suggest that they feel anything at all.

Schizoid clients may hear confrontation as a thinly veiled command that must be obeyed. I once – gently, I thought – told a new client who arrived fifteen minutes early that I didn't have a waiting room and that I normally worked with my clients until ten minutes to the hour, so that if she rang the bell during a session I wouldn't answer it. The following week I waited for half an hour and then decided to go for a walk as I gathered that she wasn't going to turn up. When I got down to the front door (I worked in a flat at the top of the house) there she was. I asked her why she hadn't rung the bell; she replied that I had told her not to ring the bell and to be on time.

The less well-functioning schizoid often has paranoid features that are expressed in rather screwy thinking. This needs to be challenged but not confronted. Humour is useful here but if that is not your strong suit just think about how you might deal with a child who claims to have seen elves sitting on the window sill or monsters under the bed. In other words, acknowledge that *they* really saw them but let them know that *you* really don't see them.

Be careful about using expressions of concern about the client's behaviour. These can be experienced by schizoid clients as either being about *your* fears or as trying to take a relationship – even a destructive one – away from the client. I learnt never to express my concern about Ruth's drinking (see Chapter Four), no matter how concerned I really did feel. These interventions can also be heard as 'mind-reading', leaving the client to feel anxious that the therapist can see something that they either can't see or are not yet ready to reveal.

Having said that, it has been my experience that schizoid clients tend to speak in code and it is the therapist's job to learn to read it. Nigel used to talk a great deal about opera and the musical theatre. During the 'trust building' phase of our work I let him do this and expressed my own interest and opinions. Later, I gently helped him to connect his references to characters on the stage to parts of himself. It was several more years before he was able to make these connections for himself. He now regularly uses stage characters to explain how he is feeling or how he has changed. The difference is that he knows that he is doing this.

I was helped in my work with Nigel by having a shared interest in opera and musicals so that I was able to read between the lines. When this isn't the case I sometimes find it helpful to ask clients to look at the pictures I have on the wall of my consulting room and to tell me a story about what they see. This is experienced as far less threatening than talking about themselves.

Nigel is now able to articulate his fear of letting me get too close to him. He says he still feels tense when he comes to our sessions. He – half-jokingly – says that I am weakening his resolve. Recently he told me about a dream he'd had, never before having done so. He was about to be knighted by the queen and he was terrified of being broken in two by the sword so that everyone could see that he was really empty inside.

It becomes easy to see why relationships with people are so threatening to people with a schizoid way of being in the world. They often feel more comfortable with fantasizing about relationship as opposed to actually having one. They also can satisfy their need for relationship through relationships with animals or inanimate objects like computers where they can have the illusion of being in control. What appear to be addictions also allow for relationship by proxy and for the illusion of being safely out of control.

The empty core

According to Seinfeld (1991) the infant's need to be loved is first expressed as an oral need. Being deprived of love is experienced as emptiness; being loved is felt as fullness. The physiological state of emptiness resulting from hunger is translated into a psychic state of emptiness that becomes the core of the psychic structure. When there is no substitute for mother the child creates one in her imagination.

This concept of the empty core is central and necessary and has a positive, self-formative function. The child begins to try out all sorts of self-parenting first on herself and, later, through creative play. This parallels the existential principle that nothingness is the core of freedom. The futile void becomes the fertile void.

If disappointments in feeding/loving become traumatic or prolonged, the empty core that exists in us all may become the bottomless pit of the schizoid. People like this deal with emptiness in two ways The first is to eliminate all need by aloofness, self-sufficiency, isolation – emptiness becomes an ideal. The second is to strive to arrive at a state of absolute completion, fullness, and fulfilment – to extinguish all need through satisfying oneself.

Seinfeld believes that it is the intensity of schizoid hunger that accounts for the client's effort to repress it. Hunger becomes less of a need in awareness and more of an identity component. The baby no longer screams in the night. Hunger has become transformed from a need and a cry to a state of mind.

In addiction the hunger for human love returns as an irresistible, senseless impulse that is experienced as belonging to the environment rather than to the addict. It is the action of a dissociated or split self. The therapist who works only to strengthen the ego or will against an 'irresistible' impulse will guarantee that the impulse will increase in power because it will remain separate from and uninfluenced by the remaining personality. The therapist working with the food, or drug, or alcohol dependent person is often afraid to – but must – allow the client to express or permit the need for the drug.

An alliance must be formed with the part of the client that wants to be free of addiction and at the same time it must reach the secret, starving, dissociated self. The impulse has to be re-owned and not experienced as outside the self, tempting. The devil made me do it. The therapist must also empathize with that part of the client that resists the impulse, that is fearful of being overwhelmed and is willing to get along in the world by renouncing all need in order to reach the need itself. The client needs to hear that the therapist wants to help bring the hungry self back into the client's full sense of self, not to submerge his will but to strengthen her influence over her whole personality. If the schizoid feels dominated by the therapist's need for them to stop their relationship with food or alcohol, or if the therapist is seen to be taking away this important relationship, the therapy will fail. This will be covered in more detail in Chapters Four and Five.

Schizoid clients may need to hold on to a negative external relationship just the way they need to hold on to their self-punishing and critical internal relationships (introjects) because to give these relationships up means annihilation. The therapist cannot risk taking away negative introjects unless there is a secure enough internalized therapist to replace them. The same goes for addictions. Often, the compulsion turns to a healthy fascination – the problem drinker develops an interest in fine wines; a former anorexic becomes a fabulous cook – once the therapist is internalized as genuinely loving and caring.

The link between schizoid and narcissistic presentations

Fairbairn (1952) and later Guntrip (1968), who was analysed by both Fairbairn and Winnicott, put forth the object relations view that the ego seeks other people rather than the pleasure that Freud suggested it was after, and that real relationships are the building blocks of the human psyche. They see a split in the self (schizoid object relations) as characteristic of virtually all emotional or personality 'disorder'. Greenberg and Mitchell (1983), make the point that what American analysts are likely to call 'narcissism', British analysts tend to call 'schizoid disorders'. The reasons for this have to do with how psychoanalysis got re-processed in America. I'm happy to see it as one of those 'two nations divided by a common language' things. The British stand for office and the Americans run. Go figure, as they say in New York.

Kohut (1977) believed that narcissism is an essential building block of the human personality that becomes pathological only when parents fail to transform the child's developmentally appropriate 'grandiose self' ('I am perfect and a part of you') in order to help him to be separate and creative. The child then grows into a person with a split self, torn between his grandiosity and his desire to please mother and father. Kernberg (1975) sees narcissistic pathology as the result of a last-ditch attempt to heal a very early split in the self through trying – but failing – to win love and approval by performing in a certain way. Both theories rely on the concept of a split self. This makes it possible to see that there are places where the narcissistic and schizoid personality features overlap.

It has been my experience that successful therapy with more obviously narcissistic presentations will usually lead to the client becoming aware of core feelings of emptiness, unreality, alienation, and emotional withdrawal more typical of the schizoid.

When my client, Ruth (see Chapter Four), first came into therapy I remember going to supervision and describing a very successful woman who was cold, distant, and critical. She told me of a recent disappointment that she had had involving a group interview. She was given the feedback, which she had obviously committed to memory, that she appeared to be 'visibly aloof, less than warm and disturbingly uninvolved'; that in order to be offered the post she would have to be 'a person for others' and this – according to her interviewers – she most obviously was not. Ruth seemed almost defiant when she related this to me.

I saw this as a possibly narcissistic presentation and was surprised when my supervisor suggested that I think along the lines of schizoid object relations. I have been interested ever since in the connection between the two terms and how to differentiate between them clinically in order to work effectively.

Narcissistic self-process is usually characterized by feelings of superiority and entitlement, which lead the narcissistically challenged among us to feel better than others on the one hand and to be completely dependent on others for self-worth on the other. The narcissist is usually unaware of this need for others and is likely to blame others for his uncomfortable feelings, particularly anger, powerlessness, and incompetence. Both others and self are subject to punishment for weakness and inferiority. This makes relationships very complicated, as the narcissistic dance means that someone will always be better or worse than somebody else.

Both narcissists and schizoids can be paranoid. Narcissistic paranoia is more likely to do with status ('Those people over there are talking about *me*'), whereas schizoid paranoia is more to do with safety ('If I ask those people for directions they might hurt me') or fear of ridicule ('I've just done a stupid thing and everyone can see'). Both types of paranoia converge in the need to control – the narcissist in order to cover feelings of helplessness and the schizoid in order to cover a terror of vulnerability and its accompanying chaos. Both types of people share a deeply felt belief in their innate badness. Narcissists project this badness on to others, while schizoids protect themselves and others by hiding their badness through keeping their distance. Having said that, some narcissists – more often than not the 'closet narcissists' – are masochistic. They actively seek punishment from those that they also seek to control. Schizoids don't need others to punish them. They do this well all by themselves. In a nutshell, schizoids have developed the apparent absence of need in order to protect the people that they fear despise them; narcissists desperately need the very people that they actively or passively despise because they have to project their inadequacy on to others.

As a result of the contradictions in the narcissist's need for others some appear to have no need for others at all. Like the schizoid described in the *DSM* they appear to be cold and unresponsive in relation to others and seek solitary activities. Like the avoidant they confide in very few. If they have sex it is clinical and fairly unsatisfying. They may even – and this is strange indeed when held up against the stereotype of the narcissist – appear to be indifferent to praise or criticism. They give the illusion of self-sufficiency and predictability. They appear to have had their need for others surgically removed because it had become redundant and a bit irritating, like an appendix.

The critical distinction between narcissistic and schizoid withdrawal is that, where both lack the capacity for intimacy and both can only *respond* as opposed to *relate* to others, the schizoid is covering a terrified core whereas the narcissist, whose infantile rage was never humanized, lacks empathy.

Klein – Melanie, not Ralph – (1957) believed that each of us is born with a fragile, easily fragmented ego. She also believed the most primitive human fear is the fear of falling apart or disintegration. Thus, according to Klein, from the start of its life the infant uses primary defence mechanisms such as splitting, projection, and introjection to manage this fear. The result of all this defending against disintegrating is to come to see the world as either 'good' (satisfying) – or 'bad' (frustrating and withholding). Klein saw this infantile world view as connected to the 'good' and 'bad' breasts, as feeding is the earliest focal point for satisfaction/frustration. So the infant splits the good from the bad and then tries to introject the good while at the same time keeping out the bad. The good is experienced as solid; the bad is experienced as fragmenting and is projected out on to others, but the scars on the ego remain.

The ever-present threat of the bad object causes the developing ego to adopt a schizoid or split defence mechanism called projective identification. This involves a non-verbal or body knowledge that bad feelings belong to others. Ideally the baby is, let's say, angry. Mother is able to feel the baby's anger through identifying with his projections (this is the basis of empathy), and eventually she gives the anger back to the baby in a way that he can experience it as non-annihilating. Ideally, after three to four months the baby gets the felt sense that good and bad co-exist and he develops the depressive position as a result of fear of his own rage and anxiety about driving away the good. He begins to experience the loss of his omnipotence and other – usually mother – becomes whole in his eyes. As a result he begins to experience his own wholeness and the split in the developing ego is repaired.

That's the theory. In practice it doesn't go that smoothly. Excessive envy and early rage experiences can prevent the transition from the paranoid–schizoid to the depressive position altogether. Envy (see Chapter Six) destroys the good. With goodness gone only the bad remains at the core of the self. Envy is the original driving force behind narcissistic rage, and it is where the schizoid experience and primitive narcissism connect. Schizoids have cut themselves off from others in order to protect themselves and the other from their felt sense of badness. Narcissists can be understood as preferring to destroy themselves rather than to allow their success to be taken away by another. Whereas schizoid clients seem to be frozen in time and need gentle and respectful thawing in order to reconnect with the feelings that were too intense for them as children, narcissists often wear their rage as an entitlement for all the ill treatment they've had.

One way I experience the difference between narcissistic and schizoid presentations in my countertransference is that when I have more patience and tolerance with myself and the client, along with a fascination for how she can turn up week after week and appear to be getting so little from me, I know I'm working with schizoid process as opposed to when a client seems to make no progress at all and I start thinking that I should have gone to law school. The latter, more narcissistic client usually has subtle ways of letting you know that they are enjoying making you feel useless.

Annelise and the big, ugly bug

In the previous chapter I talked about the more 'social-ized' schizoid clients who may experience empathy as a trigger to regress to earlier wounding as opposed to sooth-ing. I worked for many years with a woman who was desperately lonely on the one hand, yet almost unbearably prickly on the other. She had a younger brother whom she hated and envied. She would regularly talk about how she wanted to have a relationship and I used to sit there think-ing about the joke, 'How do you make love with a porcu-pine?' The answer, if you haven't already guessed, is 'very, very carefully'. She had no close friends but a wide social circle involving lots of activities that didn't seem to give her much pleasure. She was a teacher of children with special needs, yet seemed totally insensitive to the needs of others and as sensitive to rejection. She did not think she had the recognition she deserved.

One evening, several years into our therapeutic rela-tionship, I was sitting listening to her when I noticed that just behind her on the wall was a big, ugly bug that looked like some sort of mini-crustacean with hair. I was able to appear to be looking at Annalise while at the same time keeping an eye on the bug, which eventually tired of clinging to the wall and started to head for the sofa, crawl-ing between the cushion and the frame. Instinctively I turned my full attention to the bug. I could feel Annalise's characteristic but suppressed rage that I wasn't listening to her revving up. For years the dance had gone like this: I would steal a glance at the clock, or blow my nose or in some other way attend to something else, however briefly, and she would express her hurt feelings about this. I would empathize and she would burst into tears, not the tears that come from being touched but the tears that come from terrible unhappiness. We got nowhere. My supervisor told me that Annalise had a Narcissistic Personality Disorder and that I would have to continue to be patient and empathic.

The big, ugly bug came along to save us from this painful impasse. What Annalise could not have known on the evening in question was that later that night I was going to sleep on just the same sofa on which she was sitting and into which our unsuspecting saviour had crawled. So, in that convergence of events, I did not feel compassion for Annalise. I felt irritated. Really irritated. I wanted to find and dispose of that bug. Instead of making some empathic intervention along the lines of, 'When I turn my attention away from you you feel unimportant', I said, 'Annalise, I've just seen a huge bug crawl into the sofa and I'm going to find it and put it out the window.'

She looked shocked. I found the bug, helped it on to the window ledge and returned once more to Annalise, whose lower lip was quivering. After years of me trying to meet her with empathy and compassion she'd learned her lines, and said, 'I feel unimportant' and I replied, 'In that moment, it's true, you were less important to me than that bug.' Not only did Annalise not cry, she seemed curious to know how that could be possible. So I told her. And pretty much from that day forward Annalise was a changed woman. The empathy that I had been encouraged to give her only caused her to regress, not to heal. She desperately needed me to be real with her as her mother had not been able to be real with her about her excitement over and continued interest in the new baby.

Unlike a more narcissistic client Annalise hung in there and accepted me getting it wrong for her again and again until the bug was sent to save us both. I came to admire her bravery and persistence and she eventually felt safe enough with me to express her anger and her love.

A final word about love

Nigel still struggles with expressions of love. It is now possible for him to tell me about positive feelings he has towards other women. In the past he was fearful that if he admitted to sexual feelings I might punish him for feeling good. He now can 'intellectually' consider that I care for him but says it's too risky for him to allow himself to *feel* my care. We are able to talk about his fear that I might be repelled by his love and could reject him. The truth is that I feel the most exquisite tenderness for Nigel and cherish every expression of liveliness that he has been brave enough to show me, like a new mother with baby's first smile. Most of these expressions are out of his awareness and I am careful not to spoil them by calling them to his attention. I show him how I feel for him and how I instinctively respond to him through my facial expressions, which – after ten years, many of which were spent looking 'through' me – he is now able to receive and to return.

Note

1. The *DSM* criteria for the Schizoid Personality Disorder describe an isolated, detached and unemotional person who does not want close relationships, appears indifferent to the experience of others and takes no pleasure in activity,

even solitary activity. The schizoid as described by Guntrip (1968) and others has withdrawn from relationship as a result of the fear that his love/need is destructive. He longs for relationship on the one hand, yet is terrified of the price of being in relationship with people, preferring fantasy to reality, circuit boards or fur or food to flesh lest his innate 'badness' be discovered and revealed to the world.

CHAPTER FOUR

SOME THOUGHTS ON ADDICTION OR 'EVERYBODY BE DOIN' SOMETHIN''

I love the warnings that come with certain things I buy. You can tell the entire history of consumer dissatisfaction and ensuing lawsuits from reading the advice to the purchaser. My particular favourite came with a hairdryer I once bought that bore the caveat, 'Do not use while sleeping'. There's a story there.

This chapter comes with a sort of consumer warning based on past experience. Participants on 'The Seven Deadly Sins?' training over the years have found the day on 'Addiction' to be unsatisfying. No matter how we have changed the content or the structure of the day, the feedback is pretty much unchanged. I suspect that this feeling of being unsatisfied is as much an identification with the material as a comment on the quality of teaching and information.

The whole area of addiction is problematic. Many of my colleagues who work in private practice have made the decision that they will not work with alcohol and drug related problems. They say that they don't have specialized training to do so, but I suspect that the real reason is that working with people who are on some level deadening – or even killing – themselves through substance abuse leads to a deadening of the therapist that is difficult to sustain in private practice without the support of a team. As a

supervisee recently said, the therapist can't bear feeling the
level of defeat and frustration that is part and parcel of
working with addictions.

My aim here is to introduce you to some ways of thinking about and working with addictive behaviour and to
illustrate how I think about and work with it, using examples from my practice. I am not a specialist in the area of
addiction. I just have some experience of working with it,
particularly with clients who find it hard to live a life well
that includes a relationship with alcohol. If you are left
feeling unsatisfied, be interested in that feeling, look at it
in your own therapy or supervision, and remember it the
next time you feel it in the presence of a client. Therapists
who work with addiction have to fight against the feelings
of emptiness that they often must feel long before their
clients are able to.

'Everybody be doin' somethin'

I was introduced to working with addictions as a trainee
in New York, where I worked in a trade union-based
Employee Assistance Programme that provided psychotherapy and social work services to municipal employees
and their families. During the orientation week for all
trainees I went to a talk given by a woman called Frances,
the head of the Substance Abuse Team, who recounted the
statistics concerning the percentage of clients who sought
help from the EAP who were addicted to alcohol or drugs
– something like 80%. One of my fellow trainees said that
this high rate of 'addicts' must have been specific to the
population served by the unit who were what the director
referred to as 'the working poor'. Surely, my colleague

went on, you wouldn't find such a high rate of addictive behaviour in the wider population. Frances pulled herself up to her full height, looked the trainee straight in the eye and said, 'Honey, let me tell you: everybody be doin' somethin'!' Of all the things I was told in that first week that's the one I remember and that now, twenty-something years later, can say is the most true. Whether it is sex or work or booze or drugs or, these days, surfing the net, it would seem that most folks *do* be doin' something.

What do you do? Just take a moment to check how you responded to that question. How willing would you be to share what you might be able to admit to yourself with your colleagues? Would you be all right about admitting to using recreational drugs? Could you be honest about how much you *really* drink? Or do you have a 'secret' habit?

For example, I have a colleague who takes Anadin Extra to get her through the day. She first started taking them for stress headaches and then found that they not only took care of her headache but also gave her a bit of a boost when she was feeling groggy. She soon found that the headaches she was getting mid-morning – probably due to low blood sugar – were appearing at other times of the day. She took another pill. When her youngest child left home she found herself filling the void with more work. More work led to more stress, which led to more headaches, which led to her taking even more pills. She knows that she needs to work fewer hours, to eat more regularly, to get more exercise but work has become a salve to her feelings of emptiness and a boost to her self-esteem. She no longer takes Fridays off. She takes on more work and she takes more pills. Has she got a problem? Is she an addict?

My friend Maura, who has been a member of AA for over twenty years, says yes. In Maura's view my colleague has 'lost the power of choice'. Maura, who started drinking heavily after the break-up of a relationship just before her thirtieth birthday, believes that – even after twenty-two years of abstinence and sobriety – she would revert to problem drinking that would lead to her death if she ever had another drink. And she believes that the only thing that keeps her from having that next drink is regular attendance at meetings and 'working the steps'.

Liv, on the other hand, spent three months in the early 1990s at a treatment centre for cocaine addiction compounded by recreational alcohol abuse. After her stay at the centre she was told that she would need to attend NA or AA meetings at least once a day for the rest of her life if she wanted to live. She did this for several years, until she met a man and went travelling in various remote locations around the world. Her 'sponsor' at NA/AA warned her against doing this, as she was unlikely to be able to stick to her routine of morning and evening meetings in Nepal. She went anyway. One night, having returned to Kathmandu after a two-week trek, she was offered a beer, which she drank without thinking. She waited for the demons she had been warned against to take over. Nothing happened. The beer tasted good, satisfied her thirst and she didn't want a second one when it was offered. Ten years on Liv is a successful solicitor who has a relatively normal relationship with alcohol. She doesn't drink every day. Occasionally she drinks too much socially. She never drinks when she is on her own.

Liv is happy with the way she manages her drinking. Maura says that it is only a matter of time before Liv's desperate attempts at control will fail and alcohol will get the better of her. Both Liv and Maura have had many years of psychotherapy. Maura says that Liv's therapist only colludes with her problem by supporting her belief that she hasn't got a problem. Who is right?

Society self-righteously stigmatizes addiction or, what I prefer to call, 'overdoing'. There is an unwritten code of acceptability of excess. Drug use is generally frowned upon but some drugs are more socially acceptable than others and some don't even get a look-in in the hierarchy. People who work too hard are admired even if they, secretly, can't stop and put their commitment to work above their commitment to their families and their health.

Why?

The facts are that we really don't understand much about addiction and that nothing is very successful in treating it. Research has shown that only 10–30% of people who enter abstinence-based alcohol treatment programmes succeed in the long term (Heather & Robertson, 1997).The majority of alcoholics, drug addicts, over-eaters and smokers will return to their addictions within a year or two after treatment (Hunt & Matarazzo, 1973). Research into what supports people in making and sustaining a change in their behaviour shows that failure and relapse are integral parts of the cycle of change (Prochaska & DiClemente, 1986). The average person who wants to stop smoking will make three or four serious attempts over 7–10 years before they make it to long-term maintenance (Prochaska, Velicer, DiClemente, Guadagnoli, & Rossi, 1991).

Addiction or compulsive overdoing, although often described by overdoers as a way of coping with external pressures, may be seen to be a reasonably predictable reaction to emotional or physical discomfort that is in some way anticipated as being satisfying yet is ultimately unsatisfying and, in some way, 'costly'. Cost can be measured in various ways such as loss of control, relationships, money, enjoyment, or health but it must be true that on some level the ability of the substance or activity to soothe or to numb, however temporarily, outweighs the 'cost' to some extent. In other words people will continue to engage in addictive behaviour as long as they believe that it does something for them that nothing or no one else can.

The development of addictive/compulsive behaviours is explained by various people in various ways. Freud (1917) saw addictions as the result of developmental arrest; Kohut (1987) believed that addictive behaviour was an attempt – however misguided – at self-repair; Jellinek (1960) believed that addiction was an illness stemming from genetic predisposition.

If we see addictions as 'diseases' we miss, I believe, their primary function in a person's relationship to self, other, and environment. People become addicted to an experience or feeling state, not just to a substance or activity. The cycle of addiction starts because the experience of the substance or the behaviour feels good. Therapists who view addictive behaviour as self-harm often find it hard to hold in mind that just because a client says he wants to stop doing something that he or others say is bad for him doesn't mean it is not the central pleasurable relationship in his life.

Turning to a substance for comfort can also be seen as a person's best effort at self-medication for intense emotional states that have been dissociated or split off as a result of exposure to sudden trauma, such as a train crash or natural disaster, or to repeated, sustained abuse in childhood (see Chapter Eight).

People are vulnerable to addiction when they experience the loss of another through death or separation. Those with low self-esteem that keeps them from engaging in satisfying activities are also vulnerable. So, too, are those who experience 'ordinary' life transitions, such as a child leaving home or retirement. In other words, most of us, if deprived of the support of family and friends, denied rewarding activities, under stress or in other ways challenged by unpredictable circumstances, would be more vulnerable to developing an addiction or a compulsive activity. No one really seems to know why.

Current research (www.utexas.edu/research/asrec) shows that what we call addictions are closer to obsessive–compulsive disorder (OCD) and emerge in those with variations from the norm in the mesolimbic dopamine system, which subconsciously affects the frontal cortex, producing a pathological impairment in decision making. In other words, the use of addictive substances is not under the conscious control of certain individuals.

Further research in the area of affective neuroscience has discovered the concept of state dependent learning. In other words, what is 'learnt' under traumatic conditions gets dissociated or split off and is only accessible in a mental state similar to the one in which the memory was laid down. The disinhibiting effect of certain drugs or alcohol can strongly facilitate the 'reliving' of such experiences. The more similar are the context and stimuli to conditions at the time of the original trauma, the more likely the probability of remembering or, at least, re-enacting the traumatic event (van der Kolk, 1989).

This would explain two different clinical presentations in people who are doing something they want, or know they ought, to stop doing. In the first instance the over-doer is aware of experiencing an unpleasant sensation and of responding to it by having a cigarette, or a drink, or a fix. In the second, the sensation is not experienced but is projected into the environment. The client dissociates. She feels tempted, possessed by a force outside the self, as opposed to being in conflict with a desire or need that is experienced internally. The latter addictive process is much more difficult to treat, as the responsibility to use the substance has been, often subtly, attributed to the environment. People describe this in various ways but the language usually conjures up some form of possession.

It may have been Jung's observation of the addict behaving as one possessed that led him to advise the founders of Alcoholics Anonymous (AA) to fight 'spirits' with spirituality (*spiritum contra spiritus*). The second of AA's twelve steps to sobriety requires turning to a higher power: 'we came to believe that a Power greater than ourselves could restore us to sanity.'

Alcoholics Anonymous

Alcoholics Anonymous was started in the 1930s by two men whose lives were on the brink of ruin due to their excessive and obsessive drinking. It is now the most successful self-help programme ever and its Twelve Step approach requires the 'addict' to admit that he is power-less over alcohol and to turn to a 'higher power' for help to stay sober 'one day at a time'. AA now has spin-offs for drug addicts (NA), food addicts (OA), sex addicts (SA) and even for people who are 'addicted' to living with addicts (Alanon).

Alcoholics Anonymous has as its central tenet that alcoholism is a disease for which abstinence is the only remedy. I am careful to say 'remedy' and not 'cure', as members of AA believe that they are and always will be addicts. Participants introduce themselves saying, 'I'm Jim and I'm an alcoholic'. The group then responds in chorus, 'Hi, Jim'. There is no interpersonal interaction in the formal part of AA meetings. That is left for after the meeting. Meetings follow a specific format, beginning with the AA 'prayer', 'Grant me the serenity to accept the things I cannot change; the courage to change the things I can and the wisdom to know the difference'. After that someone, chosen in advance, takes 'the chair' and shares with the meeting his or her story of hitting 'rock bottom' and getting and staying sober through 'working the programme'. Members of the group then share their drinking stories; how they came to realize that they were powerless over alcohol (or drugs) and turned to a Higher Power to help them to stay sober 'one day at a time'. All stories are addressed to the 'chair'.

If you live in an urban area there are literally hundreds of AA meetings available to attend each week. Apart from the almost on-demand support of the meetings, members work with a sponsor, an alcoholic who has been 'in recovery' for several years. (The twelfth step is to help another alcoholic stop drinking.) No money changes hands except for contributions towards the coffee and hiring the venue. It is a worldwide organization run by recovering alcoholics for other alcoholics. I've got a house in rural France and, according to a neighbour, the local AA meeting consists of himself and two others who meet each week in order to stay sober and to provide a place for visiting alcoholics to meet during the holidays. In July and August and over the Christmas and Easter periods it is packed.

The anonymous nature of AA membership makes it difficult to conduct any valid research into its long-term effects. Certainly one if its more obvious short-term benefits is that it immediately replaces the drinker's social or solitary activity with a fellowship of other recovering alcoholics who can provide support for maintaining abstinence. In addition, AA culture offers, in the form of catch-phrases like 'one day at a time', 'let go and let God', 'this too shall pass', the rapid assimilation of self-soothing and coping skills that can be employed in the space between meetings. Finally, it offers total acceptance. No drinking story is too terrible to be told.

In my experience of working with people who are involved in twelve step programmes I have sometimes had to confront a philosophical clash that is difficult for me to manage, in that the gestalt therapist in me believes in personal responsibility and my psychoanalytic roots have shown me again and again that one's relationship with self, others, and the environment changes when one's ability to choose is combined with making what has been unconscious conscious. This flies in the face of AA's insistence that problem drinkers are powerless over alcohol, that only a power outside themselves keeps them sober, and that problem drinking is a sign of a deeper moral decay that 'dooms' the drinker who does not remain abstinent.

My friend Maura peppers her social conversations with reference to herself as an alcoholic, and regularly tells stories about her drinking days, even though she hasn't had a drink in twenty-two years. I tell her that she has never stopped having a relationship with alcohol; that being sober has become her new obsession. She replies, 'I'm an addict. What do you expect?'

In my opinion AA's success is dependent on keeping ex-drinkers involved in the game 'alcoholic' (Berne, 1964). It can also become the new 'drug of choice'. People who use twelve step programmes to remain abstinent often seem to switch positions on the 'drama triangle' (Karpman, 1968). The alcoholic (victim) becomes the recovering alcoholic (rescuer). Alcohol remains the persecutor, ever-present in even the non-drinker's lived experience.

Having said that, AA is a powerful force in many people's journey to abstinence or better management, and I strongly urge therapists who work with clients who are members of AA or other twelve step programmes to attend an 'open meeting' in order to be able to work with and not against some of the core beliefs that the client will have introjected. Information about how to find a schedule of open meetings in your area can be obtained from AA's general office.

Motivational interviewing

A new approach to treating addiction, developed by Miller (see www.motivationalinterview.org), is surpassing the twelve step approach for in-patient treatment in the USA, partly because health insurance companies have taken the view that Motivational Interviewing is a more effective in-patient treatment than programmes based on a twelve step approach. I wonder if this is because people who stop drinking or using drugs are supported to arrive at their own motivation for doing so.

Motivational Interviewing is a therapeutic technique and set of principles that is consistent with humanistic philosophies, as it takes a paradoxical view of change that is supported by current research.

Motivational Interviewing begins with the premise that motivation is the key to any long-term behavioural change and that change will occur when the drinker, or smoker, or drug user sees that the advantages of altering their behaviour outweigh the disadvantages. In developing this approach Miller made two observations: that if one person pushes for one side of an argument the other person will tend to take the other side; and that if we say something often enough we will come to believe it.

The practice of Motivational Interviewing is directive and client centred. Its goal is to help the client to examine and to resolve ambivalence. It does not involve direct persuasion or behavioural challenge, nor does it offer information about the problem itself or coping strategies. Its philosophy is that change is a product of interpersonal interaction and the relationship between therapist and client is one that respects the client's autonomy and freedom of choice along with its consequences.

In practice, the therapist needs to strive to understand the client's frame of reference; to express acceptance of the client and his behaviour along with affirmation of his freedom to choose the direction of his own life; to elicit and to reinforce *the client's own* expressions of problem recognition, concern, and the desire for and belief about his ability to change; to keep pace with the client and to not generate resistance by jumping ahead of him.

Research (Orford & Keddie, 1986) has shown that treatment that allows the client to choose his own route, based on his own values, to altering his relationship with alcohol – either through abstinence or controlled drinking – is the most successful. They remind us that 'successful' abstinence may be viewed as the number of days in a certain period that the client abstains from drinking rather than total, life-long abstinence, as is the focus of twelve step programmes.

The hardest and the single most important thing I've learned as a therapist who works with people who overdo is never to suggest to them that they need to change their behaviour nor to enthusiastically agree with them when they reach that decision on their own. This is pretty hard when a client tells you horror stories – often tantalizingly – about the risks she takes with her health. But I can swear from my own experience (which research would seem to support) that, whatever their 'poison', clients who become abstinent or who become able to change their relationship with what they once did too much of, have only done so when I have been rigorous about refusing to work directly with the behaviour and have also gone so far as to accept and defend it as a part of who they are. This is a deliberate clinical intervention and is different from ignoring it altogether out of fear or ignorance.

A model for change

Research into treating addictive behaviours (Prochaska & DiClemente, 1986) shows that different people need to approach their relationship to their problem at different levels. Some need to change their behaviour, others their thinking; others need to change their relationships to their family or social network while others need to resolve intrapsychic conflicts. Prochaska and DiClemente believe that clinical intervention needs to begin at the level of awareness that the client brings to the treatment,

combined with what the psychotherapist's clinical assessment and judgement can support. They offer a model that
can help the therapist to assess the client's level of awareness of the problem and/or their motivation to change it.

Prochaska and DiClemente see change as a process. In
the 'pre-contemplation' stage the client may be aware that
he has a problem but has not considered doing anything
about it. Clients who are 'sent' to therapy by a concerned
employer or partner are often in this stage, where they
have very little awareness of how their substance abuse is
affecting them and those around them. This phase is
called denial in AA. I am not interested in working in
private practice with clients who are at this stage in the
change process. Both the problem and the cause of the
problem are projected into the environment. 'The devil
makes me do it.' The work in therapy needs to be towards
helping the client to re-own the impulse rather than to
grow in strength to be able to resist it. The therapist who
focuses on controlling the behaviour before the client is
able to own it as hers may find that the compulsion to
drink grows rather than fades. The process of re-owning
the impulse inevitably must include allowing the client to
passionately express their apparent need for their drug of
choice (for food see Chapter Five)

Ian, an architect, was referred to me by an Employee
Assistance Programme (EAP). He was a committed and
defensive drinker. He thought it was 'a bit naughty' to
stop off for a Bacardi Breezer as a pick-me-up on the way
to work after a heavy night but he still did so regularly. He
had been told that he smelt of drink in the mornings and
that clients and colleagues had noticed this when he
appeared a bit the worse for wear. In fact he had failed to
turn up for important on-site meetings on more than one

occasion. He agreed to come to see me as he thought it would look better 'for work'. He denied that drinking was a problem for him. It was more of a problem for others. In his view it was perfectly understandable that he drank. Everybody drinks under pressure. And the client always expects a boozy lunch after a meeting.

I did not see Ian as a candidate for psychotherapy and told him so. Several months later he phoned to make another appointment and he is coming regularly to therapy. Having been diagnosed with liver problems he was beginning to accept that drinking could kill him, even though he still was reluctant to admit that *he* had a problem. Nevertheless, he had begun to think about doing something about his drinking. One could imagine that this shift came about because his motivation to live was beginning to be stronger than his motivation to keep on drinking. He had moved into the 'contemplation' phase.

The 'contemplation' phase is characterized by a certain amount of ambivalence about making a change. These clients are 'on the fence'. They may be able to see both the benefits and the drawbacks of changing but the benefits are often expressed as outside the self, as in, 'My doctor will stop hassling me if I cut down on my drinking'. Clients in this phase often talk about stopping or cutting down sometime in the future. 'I'll give up after Christmas. Most people detox then so it won't be so difficult.'

Clients in the contemplation phase also engage in a process that I see as similar to Kubler-Ross's (1969) 'bargaining' phase. Ian began to admit that the amount of spirits he was drinking (a litre a day) was excessive. 'Right then,' he said. 'It's only wine from now on for me.' When working with clients who are in the contemplation phase I try to remember that there is a part of the client who sees me as someone who can help them to 'get better' as well as a part that believes that I can fix it so they can keep on drinking or using drugs without ill consequence. Part of them is becoming increasingly aware of the 'cost' of their behaviour while another part firmly believes that therapy can offer a miracle cure. There is a narcissistic quality to this belief. Johnson (1987) talks about the narcissist who presents for therapy as doing so once he begins to experience troubling symptoms that challenge his 'false self'. Rather than wanting to reach the 'real self' he wants to get back to the way he was before the symptoms started. I have found it helpful with clients in this stage to empathize with their desire to be special. I may also gently share my own struggles with needing to accept my limitations as well as to name and to gently dissolve their fantasy that I can cure them without any action on their part. In my experience, clients who struggle with overdoing hold a deep-seated belief that therapy will be able to help them to become 'normal' drinkers. This is usually not the case, probably due to the hard-wiring that is laid down in the brain and how it is programmed to interact with alcohol under certain conditions. Problem drinkers *can* become 'controlled' drinkers but the price may be eternal vigilance and the probability of relapse or, at least, loosening of control from time to time.

Ian did stop drinking after Christmas, but after a few weeks started again. I empathized that he had done something that was much more difficult than he had anticipated, had done the best he could, and might need to look at some of the difficulties he encountered. With clients who have reached the 'preparation' phase the work is often to help them to experience their dilemma, which is wanting to be untouchable while also fearing that they are not.

Clients who are in the 'preparation' phase have taken some ownership of the benefits of changing and of the difficulties that they will encounter. They may have experimented with making the change through having survived periods of abstinence or controlled use of the substance. They are open to looking at what support they might need from the therapist and from the environment in order to make the change. Smoking or drinking or using drugs does take up rather a lot of time, and clients may need to look at how they will fill up the space that is made when they stop doing something they are used to doing. They also may need to imagine themselves in social situations in order to identify how they will feel without a drink or a cigarette to prop them up.

It is at this point in the therapy that the therapist is in danger of becoming allied with other people in the client's life who want him to stop doing what they're doing. After his first attempt to stop drinking, Ian spent about three months in therapy focusing alternatively on complaining about his wife and on making preparations to 'give up the booze forever, damn it'. His wife eventually issued him an ultimatum: to choose between his drinking and his marriage after a particularly disastrous holiday abroad. I empathized with the hard choice he had to make between his wife and his drinking. As crazy as it may seem to someone who has not battled with an addiction, in the client's mind the choice seems nearly impossible to make as each side of the decision involves almost unbearable loss and incomprehensible difficulty. The client will only be able to move into the 'action' phase when the therapist is able to help him to experience the degree of loss and difficulty that faces him whatever choice he makes.

It is difficult for therapists who have not struggled with overdoing to understand just how hard it is to stop. Oliver, who hasn't had a drink in ten years, went through two weeks this summer of 'shaking and sweating' and feeling as if he would 'kill for a drink' for no apparent reason. Mercedes has not smoked a cigarette for over thirty years, but is still occasionally 'nearly overcome by the desire to smoke'. Only remembering what a struggle it was to quit in the first place keeps them from giving in to their urges.

In the 'action' phase clients have made a significant change and will need to be supported for doing well and to deal with the feelings that will no doubt have arisen. Mourning is an important part of this phase, and the therapist needs to remember that although a client has stopped doing something that may have been 'bad' for him he will miss it and may even find it difficult to remember the bad times that led him to make the change. The therapist needs to be respectful of the client's often idealized view of his drinking days, to remember that any change is progress, and to be careful not to collude with the client's suggestions that they've cracked the problem.

Ian missed drinking terribly, even though he accepted that it was going to kill him and that he would lose his family on the way. The only emotion he ever expressed powerfully was profound sadness. He sobbed and sobbed when I set up an experiment in which he could say good-bye to his 'old friend'. It was moving and shocking to see the grip that alcohol had on this man.

'Maintenance' and 'relapse' are the final two phases and I see them as connected. What I like about Prochaska and DiClemente's model is that they assume that relapse is a part of the change process; relapse is to be expected – even prepared for – and accepted as normal. I once asked Thich Nhat Hanh, a Zen master, how we could know what enough was. He replied that a baby does not know that he will learn to walk but the mother does. Mother, he said, needs to laugh lovingly at the baby when he falls down and gets frustrated and cries. Mother can do this, he said, because mother knows that all this falling down and knocking over tables *is* the baby learning to walk. I find this image useful when working with clients who are struggling to be free of overdoing. Having said that, I find the self-defeating aspects of denial and relapse hard to manage and only accept clients like Ian when the balance of my practice allows me to have the psychological space to hold in mind that my work with other clients is more rewarding.

Once Ian was able to accept what he called 'defeat', we looked at strategies to maintain his alcohol-free life. He goes to a weekly support group where he has made friendships with other people who don't drink and he is able to call on them when he feels tempted to 'fall off the wagon'. He has negotiated a plan with his wife in case he does – and he probably will – fall off the wagon and now has her support in his journey to sobriety rather than just her fury. Ian was someone who refused to consider AA because of its emphasis on a 'higher power'. I have gently guided him towards Thich Nhat Hanh's (1987) *Miracle of Mindfulness*, which makes Zen meditation practices accessible to Westerners. He teaches people to 'meditate' while walking to work or doing the washing-up, and has helped people like Ian to call on the spirit inside himself to support him when he feels in need of support and is on his own.

Ruth – 'Living well is the best revenge'

I have concentrated so far on work with a client who had very little initial awareness of his drinking as a problem, who had very low motivation for change, and who really never did gain much awareness of the dynamics of his relationship with alcohol, self, and others. I want to focus now on the client with a good deal of insight who did not come into therapy to stop drinking, but who revealed a problem with drink once the 'working alliance' was in place.

Clients whose self-process is on the schizoid end of the continuum may be reluctant to reveal an 'addiction' to the therapist because they fear that the therapist may want to take it away. Seinfeld (1991) recommends that an alliance must be formed with the part of the client that wants to be free of addiction as well as with the part that is starving and is experienced by the client not as need but as temptation. The client needs to believe that the therapist wants to help bring the hungry, love-starved self back into the client's full sense of self, not to control her but to strengthen her influence over her whole personality. If schizoids feel dominated by the therapist's need for them to stop their relationship with food or alcohol, or if the therapist is seen to be taking away this important relationship, the therapy will fail.

Ruth was in her early forties when she came to see me. She originally qualified as a psychiatrist, but after three years in a large urban hospital she became disillusioned and trained as a solicitor. She spent a few unhappy years working in a City firm and now works as a freelance consultant in occupational health and employment law. She was very successful and lived for her work. She had a relationship with another woman but they did not live together and Ruth said she preferred it that way. Often they just spent weekends together.

I experienced Ruth as an intelligent, engaging, and quite beautiful woman, although this was not how she experienced herself. She was very tall, which I found striking. She believed she 'took up too much space.' She told me that she believed she needed an exorcism. My countertransference was of feeling on the one hand very drawn to this woman and, on the other, extremely anxious. This, when held against the background of her view of herself as possessed by an evil spirit, led me to respect that Ruth was a terrified infant in pseudo-competent adult packaging. It was, I believe, this early identification of a fundamentally schizoid process that helped us to work together successfully.

I had a very powerful image – almost like a film running on a split screen while Ruth was talking – of a rather mad mother taking her child to a doctor and insisting that the child was sick. I kept this to myself, making a note to remember this. I was alerted by this image that 'mother' would need to see me as a good doctor who was on her side. It would be some years before I was able to understand the terrified infant well enough to enable her to emerge in the room. For the most part I felt invited to collude with 'mother' and 'professional Ruth' that this client was very sick and needed fixing. I somehow managed most of the time to appear engaged with Ruth but unruffled by her efforts to convince me of how sick and unlovable she was.

When, after several months of therapy, Ruth could see that she was getting nowhere in convincing me that she was really a hopeless case, she began to talk about her relationship with alcohol. This could be seen on the one hand as Ruth's upping the ante and trying to convince me that she really *was* sick or – and this is how I chose to see it – as her expressing enough trust in me to believe that she could reveal this aspect of herself without fearing that I would try to take it away.

Ruth revealed that she often drank 'to the point of no return'. She did this alone at night. She drank a bottle of wine most evenings with dinner but, for no reason that she was aware of, sometimes opened another bottle and drank that and more until she passed out. As far as she was aware no one but her partner knew about this. Ruth, who presented as someone who was very much in control of her emotions and her life, felt deep shame about this 'weakness'.

Schizoid clients may need to hold on to a negative external relationship just the way they need to hold on to their self-punishing and critical internal relationships (introjects) because to give these relationships up means facing an intolerable void. The therapist cannot risk taking away negative introjects unless there is a secure enough internalised therapist to replace them.

I began to see Ruth's relationship with alcohol as an externalization of her relationship with her mother. Ruth was 'a bit of an afterthought'. Her brothers were eight and ten when she was born. Her father was 'not really around much'; her mother was very involved in charitable and social causes and did not have much time for Ruth. 'My mother was a saint,' she said. Her eyes looked haunted and her body was rigid.

In the five years that we had worked together I never worked directly with Ruth's drinking but, rather, attempted to contact and to hold in various ways the frightened, angry, unloved child. As Ruth gradually came to trust me, I gently introduced my clinical thinking about the 'witch mother'. By this I mean the damaged, envious, and destructive pole of the 'sainted mother' (Kalsched, 2003). As I have come to understand it, these mothers defend against their own badness and madness by over-identifying with the 'saint' polarity. Their 'badness' is then projected on to their baby, often from birth. These are mothers who do not believe they can produce anything good and convey that belief unconsciously to their child.

Fairbairn (1952) believed that the child of such a mother becomes 'bad' in order to keep the parent(s) 'good': 'The child takes upon himself the burden of badness . . . it is better to be a sinner in a world ruled by God than to live in a world ruled by the Devil' (pp. 109–110).

In my experience, the 'witch mother' does not overtly treat her child badly. On the contrary, she often appears to be doing everything possible for the child's welfare. Often the child is over-protected on the one hand and unprotected on the other. As a child Ruth was not allowed to run too fast or to gallop on her pony, but was often left in the care of nannies and rather sadistic-sounding relations. The conflicting messages at a psychological level are 'You are precious and must be careful' on the one hand and 'You are too much for me and I don't care what happens to you' on the other.

When I was working with Ruth I remembered Fairbairn's warning that becoming aware of the internalized bad mother was not nearly as difficult as giving up one's 'devotion' to her. I began to see Ruth's negative self-image, combined with her drinking, as evidence of Ruth's devotion to mother.

One day, when Ruth was in the middle of a self-hating litany, I became aware of a particularly vicious presence. I took a risk and said, 'That's crazy. Only a sick, sadistic, mad mother would think that about her own child. You get out of here right now and leave Ruth alone.'

I looked shocked, Ruth looked shocked, and I could almost hear the door slam as mother left the room. We sat in silence until Ruth finally said, looking like an excited four-year-old, 'Blimey!'

Seinfeld believes that it is necessary to confront the sadistic thinking in clients who also engage in self-destructive behaviour. He sees it as potentially life saving (Seinfeld, 1991, p. 155).

After 'standing up to' Ruth's mother, things improved dramatically for Ruth. In the sessions she became more animated in her exploration of her past, particularly about her relationship with her mother. There was much more energy in the room, although I don't think she was particularly aware of feeling anything except for 'more alive'. Months went by without Ruth reporting drinking too much – in fact she didn't berate herself for anything. Intellectually, she was beginning to connect to the idea that she had been hated and envied as a child and I was able to offer her my hypotheses about her infancy; about how her experience of feeding and nappy changing laid down in her – almost from the start of her life – a felt sense of being too much and unwelcome.

Together we basked in this new level of exploration. Then, I made a mistake. At least, at the time it was experienced by both of us as a mistake. Ruth had been talking about her partner, who had been going through a difficult time looking after her dying father. In what turned out to be a complete misattunement I said something like, 'She really needs you to be there for her at the moment.'

Ruth didn't respond overtly but I could feel her rage. It was towards the end of the session and I decided not to own up to my obvious blunder. I didn't see her again for nearly four months. She left a message on my answering machine after not turning up for her session the following week that said that she'd had the row of all rows with her partner and had broken her finger. She said she was obviously getting worse, that I refused to recognize that she *was* an alcoholic, that she was going to join AA and that I was not to try to persuade her to come back to see me. So I didn't. But, interestingly, I had some sense that this was what she needed to do: to be furious with me and to punish me and to see me survive. I needed, in the transference, to be the 'mother' who could let her down *and* survive her rage.

Eventually Ruth phoned and asked to see me. She said that in the time – four months – she'd been away she'd been through somewhat of a transformation. She had gone to AA, regularly attending one meeting a week. She had done everything she could to embrace the culture – got a sponsor, started working the steps, shared at meetings. She said she had to fight all the time against her feeling that she wasn't like the others, but listened to her sponsor, who told her that that was just her 'disease' talking. One day at her regular weekly meeting only a few people turned up so that everyone had an opportunity to share. Ruth was the only one who hadn't spoken and she said, ' I'm not sick. I'm *not!*', and left the meeting.

When she first came to see me and for the first few years of the therapy, Ruth drank every day, although not always, in her eyes, excessively. After returning to therapy after the 'rupture' and her period of abstinence in AA she decided to start drinking again, but not during the week, and mostly kept to this plan without difficulty. Weekends, when her partner was travelling, were still potential crisis times and, from time to time, Ruth over-indulged.

The bad times were fewer and less dramatic and Ruth was more able to learn from her lapses as opposed to using them to beat herself up. She also was able to see that her out-of-control drinking tended to be triggered when she went felt lonely, particularly if she had a problem, or even a success, that she wanted to share with someone. She also came to see that she would 'punish' herself by drinking too much when she believed she had done something wrong.

I became much more aware of the 'child' in this extremely articulate and capable woman who, it appeared, felt that she had done something for which she could never be forgiven. The more we had been able to metaphorically, if not kill, but quiet the 'witch', the more this 'guilty' little girl screamed to be attended to.

Ruth's dream life, which had over the years in various ways produced images of a mother who refused to die, began to change. One day she came feeling very disturbed by a dream in which she had gone to check on a flat that she had not lived in for some time to discover that she had left two cats inside who had, in their desperation to be fed, destroyed all the furniture with their claws and their excrement but were somehow still alive. She felt overcome with dread and guilt when she thought about having somehow forgotten the kittens and leaving them in such a starving state for so long. Ruth seemed to quiet down when I offered her my sense that in her dream world she had come back just in time to save the kittens. Ruth was then able to make meaning of the dream and saw it as the 'child' in her saying, 'It's not too late to save me.'

The dream about the kittens marked a new phase in the therapy, where guilt was very much in focus. Yalom (1980) talks about the existential guilt that clients experience when faced with the choice to give up an addiction. He says that stopping an addictive behaviour is often accompanied by an experience of guilt about the harm that the client has been doing to herself and others that propels them back into the behaviour in order not to experience the guilt. I do not disagree that guilt often rises to the surface when a client's relationship to herself and a harmful substance changes, but I believe that the guilt has its roots in a childhood where the client regularly felt guilty for something.

Guilt is an unpopular concept in humanistic therapies. TA calls it a 'racket' feeling, gestalt sees it as one polarity of confluence. As trainees we were told only to feel guilty about something that we could do something about or make amends. This, I believe, completely misses the point that the original 'sin' was, in the client's mind, committed long ago and may not be in conscious memory. Underlying what has been 'forgotten' may also be a deeper guilt about the psychological space the client took up in the family for being 'bad' or 'different' which may be re-lived in the consulting room as a difficulty in engaging in the psychological space of the therapeutic encounter.

Following the dreams about the kittens, Ruth reconnected with two childhood memories. When she was about four she had been given a kitten to look after 'all by myself'. She woke up one morning and couldn't find the kitten. She saw that she had left her window open and ran outside to find the kitten lying on the ground under her bedroom window. She ran to her father and told him that the kitten was 'sleeping on the ground with jam on his mouth.' Father told Ruth to go to her room and somehow disposed of the corpse. Not another word was spoken about the matter but, when Ruth some years later asked for a pet, she was told she couldn't have one because she wasn't able to look after an animal. A second memory emerged at this point in the therapy. When Ruth was ten she went careering around a corner in a dark hallway leading to the kitchen and ran straight into her beloved and ageing nanny, who was carrying a tray heaped with things for tea. Nanny lay motionless on the floor and Ruth ran for help. She was told to go to her room and stay there, which she did for what seemed like ages in great distress. She heard an ambulance come and go but still nobody came to check on her. The incident was never mentioned again but every Christmas until she was fifteen Ruth was taken to a nursing home to visit nanny, who had demented as a result of the accident. She was sent in alone while her parents sat in the car.

Ruth came to realize how she had lived her life in the shadow of these and other experiences. She was also able to empathize with and to forgive the little girl in her who had not been helped to deal with her guilt and had been left, instead, with rage that she turned against herself.

Ruth had another dream. She was on an underground train with several other people, including an attractive man who sat opposite her and with whom she was flirting. An announcement came over the tannoy that someone on the train had a bomb. The train stopped at Earls Court and, just as the doors were closing, Ruth realized that the man she was flirting with had the bomb and she managed to get off the train and run up the stairs just moments before it exploded. My response to the dream was to wonder if Ruth was ready to acknowledge the explosive and destructive part of her and Ruth said, 'I think I've reached the point of no return.'

Ruth phoned just before her next appointment sounding cheerful and saying that she couldn't come to see me because she'd left the bath running the night before and that there was 'a terrible mess' she had to sort out. I commiserated and said I didn't have any alternative times to offer her and that I'd see her the following week. When I put the phone down I wondered if Ruth would punish herself for having caused the flood by drinking too much.

She arrived early for her next appointment, which she had never done before, sat in a different place from the one she normally sat in and told me that she had decided to stop drinking. The night after the flood in her flat her neighbour – who had also been affected by Ruth's overflowing bath – came round unexpectedly to thank Ruth for doing such a good job of sorting things out with the insurers and decorators. Ruth offered him a glass of wine and had one herself. When the neighbour left she had another one, and eventually finished the bottle. She was about to open another one when she heard my voice in her head saying, 'But you haven't done anything wrong.' She then opened the second bottle, poured it down the sink and went to bed.

It is now two years since Ruth made the decision not to drink any more. She now drinks socially and sparingly. She believes, and so do I, that she will not take the risk of attempting to renew her solitary relationship with alcohol by drinking alone. She says it would be like 'having good sex with someone who you know will beat you up after-wards.'

When Ruth first revealed her problem with alcohol to me she was well aware of the severity of her problem and actively believed that psychotherapy was the way for her to deal with it. She was able to modify her use of alcohol and was not physically dependent on it. She was more of a 'secret' drinker than an all-round 'problem drinker'. She had regular liver function tests. Her drinking was a prob-lem in her relationship but there were co-creational factors involved as well. Her ability to work well was not compro-mised by her drinking. She did, however, tend to drink when she *had* done something well. She had two good friends who did not drink and she was happy to be in their company and to go on holidays with them where drink did not figure much or at all. All of these factors supported me to work with her the way I did.

Although one could argue that Ruth had borderline features, her solitary drinking seemed to reflect a self-imposed exile characterized by self-punishment and a fear of reaching out as opposed to a fear of being abandoned. With a more borderline client I might have worked with the drinking more than I did with Ruth, helping the client to see that the drinking was a reaction to something that had been stirred up internally by making interven-tions such as, 'You felt anxious that your partner would leave you and used wine to soothe yourself', or 'Giving a successful speech makes you anxious that you won't need others any more so you drink to keep them near you'. With a more narcissistic client, like Ian, I tend to empathize with the difficulties and to remain more focused on the task as the client sees it as opposed to on the process or awareness.

Supervision

My focus in this chapter has been on working with clients who are either aware that they've got a problem or whose problem has caused others to be concerned. I want to say something here about helping supervisees to recognize when they may be working with a client who is seeking an addictive solution and does not admit it. These clients will often communicate their difficulties one way or another and it helps if the therapist can read their code.

I once supervised a very experienced person-centred therapist who was telling me about a new client, a solicitor in her thirties. The client had mentioned that she had recently been hospitalized for pancreatitis. My supervisee also mentioned that the first session had been interrupted ten minutes before the end by the client's minicab driver ringing the doorbell. I wondered if the client had a drink problem, as she was young to have a disease of the pancreas and most women her age who live in a county town drive to and from therapy. My colleague refused to consider this as a possibility. Several months later she told me that her client had arrived for her session that week 'pissed as a newt'. When I asked how she had handled this she replied that she had sent her away. She never saw the client again.

I believe that by coming to therapy under the influence of alcohol this client was trying to get her therapist to take her seriously. I also think that, had the therapist held in her mind the possibility that her client had a drink problem, the client on some level might have felt more 'seen' and would not have had to enact what she could not speak about. Furthermore, in my view, the therapist made a mistake by sending this client away. Of course it is not possible to conduct therapy when a client is under the influence, but they can be respected and kept safe. By so doing the therapist conveys that all of them, even the parts that they have not yet been able to speak about, are acceptable. At the next session the client's state the previous week can be discussed and meaning can be made by both client and therapist.

As supervisors we will regularly meet clients who are using alcohol or drugs excessively or even dangerously, and we need to have some framework to assess which of these can benefit from psychotherapy and which need more hands-on treatment such as detox or referral to a specialist substance abuse counsellor.

Although most people who use recreational drugs and alcohol do so socially, there are risks involved and clients who present for therapy who are concerned about their behaviour are at some level aware of this. The American Society of Addiction Medicine (www.asam.org) have produced six criteria that can be helpful in assessing whether or not psychotherapy is the most appropriate treatment. I have adapted these slightly and added a seventh category, borrowed from Rogers (1951), which is the client's availability for psychological contact.

I Detoxification/withdrawal – How physically dependent is the client on the substance? Are they able to manage periods without it? Are their withdrawal symptoms such that they need the substance for relief?

II. Physical health – Is the client's GP aware that they are regular drinkers or drug users? Is their use of the substance taking a toll on their health i.e. liver function, hepatitis A, HIV?

III. Emotional/behavioural – Is the client experiencing drug or alcohol-related paranoia or aggression? Is their use of alcohol or drugs affecting their relationships or their ability to work? Are they secretive? Have they been in trouble with the police or does their behaviour put them at risk such as driving whilst under the influence?

IV. Acceptance/resistance – How deep is their denial or their discounting of the seriousness of their drug or alcohol use? Is the client aware of the potential danger to self or others?

V. Abstinence potential – Would their physical health be compromised by sudden cessation? Are they able to be flexible in their use of drugs or alcohol?

VI. Environmental influences – How much does family and/or social life revolve around drinking or taking drugs? What are the forces in the field that support the client making a change? What forces maintain the behaviour? Does the behaviour stem from a particular psycho/social stressor such as bereavement or trauma?

VII Availability for psychological contact – Has the client got some insight into the psychological triggers for the behaviour? Can she accept some responsibility for it? Is she on some level hoping that psychotherapy will 'cure' her without some kind of effort on her part? Does she blame others for her actions?

CHAPTER FIVE

EATING DISORDERS*

The chapter headings in this book pretty much correspond to the order that we teach them on 'The Seven Deadly Sins?' training. Because of the emphasis on the course of being able to 'use' what is being evoked in us in the therapeutic relationship, we tell the participants at the beginning of each year to pay particular attention to what is evoked in them by each of the topics. It has been our experience that people have felt 'unsatisfied' at the end of the day on addiction and, if you've just read that chapter, that might be how you're feeling now. Just be prepared for how you may feel when you read this chapter. I've already been to the kitchen twice to look for something to eat. We usually find that people on the course buy chocolate at lunchtime on the day on eating disorders to have at teatime, even though biscuits are in no short supply. When we were working on the chapter for its inclusion in another book, we ate a lot of KitKats. I don't even really like chocolate.

Our aim here is to introduce you to some of the influences, developmental and cultural, that affect a client's relationship with food and with her body and then, through examples of our work over the years, to help you to identify when a client has a food-related problem, how

---

*This chapter was co-written with Penny Daintry. A version will appear in *Handbook of Person Centred Counselling*, Sage (2006).

to work with these and when to refer on or to work along-side other professionals. We urge you to seek specialist supervision when working with, or when supervising ther-apists who are working with, clients with eating problems. You may find the Eating Disorders Association website (www.edauk.com) a good place to start if you are seeking further training or access to specific information and current research.

Developmental issues

In Chapter Three we looked at the concept of the 'empty core' (Seinfeld, 1991) to help us to understand schizoid self-process. Thinking about the experiences of emptiness and fullness, and giving and taking, has helped us immea-surably in our work with clients who have complicated relationships with their bodies and with food. A baby's need to be loved is first expressed as an oral need. Being deprived of food/love is experienced as emptiness; being fed/loved is experienced as fullness. It is possible to imag-ine that the body-state of emptiness that results from not being fed is turned into a psychic state of emptiness that, in a very small baby, can feel like the very core of its newly forming self.

This 'void' is common in all human experience but, if disappointments in feeding/loving become traumatic or prolonged, the empty core or existential void that exists in us all may become the bottomless pit. There are two solu-tions to this chronic and terrifying state of emptiness. The child can withdraw from a world that is unresponsive into her fantasy world and cut off from her physical and psychic experience and become self-sufficient ('I don't need any one or any thing') or she can turn to her body and to food when it is available, and attempt to extinguish the need herself. Both of these solutions involve a turning away from human contact.

We take as a premise in our work with eating disorders and other addictive or compulsive solutions that they have some developmental origin. If you think about it, taking comes before giving in human development. The infant has to take from the breast or the bottle in order to live. Giving comes later. People with eating disorders have, we imagine, had some 'injury' to the taking–giving process. In addition they have had to turn to their own inadequate resources to feed and to soothe themselves in the absence of another.

Although eating disorders can occur at any age, we believe the ground is prepared in infancy and early child-hood. Puberty is the time when this ground gets stirred up again as the child struggles with changes in her body and with separating from her family. Problems with food are, on the surface, as varied as any other problems. The common thread that unites people with eating disorders is that they tend to feel alienated and in deep internal distress. They struggle in their relationships with self, others, and the world. To put it simply, they hate them-selves and expect others to follow suit. Their isolation and loneliness is compounded by what feels like a special and exclusive relationship with food, their body – even their symptoms – all of which serve as replacements for human contact. As a result they will not see the therapist as a likely source of comfort. They may even see the therapist as wanting to separate them from their best friend.

Clients who have lost control over their relationship with food and their bodies are usually people whose sense

109

of self is derived from the definition others give to their experience because they have no felt sense of identity. They protect themselves from a deep sense of worthlessness through blaming and controlling others, through self-disgust (they pre-empt the attack by attacking themselves), and by seeking solutions outside themselves to help them to cope with unbearable inner pain and emptiness. Their relationship with food is used to deaden what they believe are 'unacceptable' feelings, such as anger, rage, jealousy, envy, unhappiness, and depression. Clients with complicated relationships with their bodies and with food are likely to present as nice, compliant, helpful and, often, ingratiating.

The literature about the causes of and clinical solutions for eating disorders is vast and can be confusing and contradictory. Crisp (1989) sees anorexia as a way of coping with the challenges of adolescence –to him puberty is the villain that sets in motion an avoidance of development. Lacey (1986) is more specific about stresses in adolescence such as parental marital conflict, academic striving, poor peer group relations and carbohydrate-abstinent dieting as precipitating factors, particularly of bulimia. Duker and Slade (1988) focus on how starvation and/or bingeing and purging create changes in the personality of the sufferer. Feminist writers such as Orbach (1982), Bloom (1987), and Wolf (1991) offer a socio-cultural perspective; and Minuchin, Rosman, and Baker (1978), Palazzoli (1986), and Bruch (1974) offer insights into the family dynamics. For the most part in this chapter we will rely on our own clinical experience and on what our clients have taught us.

Although none of the examples that follow is of work with male clients, we do want to say that 10% of people with eating disorders are male and of that group 20% are gay men. Men who develop eating problems are likely to do so as a result of having been bullied for being fat kids or as a result of pressure – and this is particularly true of gay men – to have the body beautiful. Men who need to control their weight because of their vocation, like jockeys and athletes, are also susceptible to problems that begin with regular and often drastic work-related dieting.

In our experience of working with eating disorders in all of their variety and complexity, an impaired relation-ship with food is invariably related to ruptures in the client's history of tactile and emotional 'feeding'. A person's relationship with food is symbolic of early devel-opmental and relational issues. Winnicott (1989), who was a paediatrician as well as a psychoanalyst, described mother's job as introducing and reintroducing baby's mind and body to each other. His theories are supported by current research in affective neuroscience (Schore, 2001; see Chapter Eight). Mother does this by respond-ing to the baby's bodily sensations and feelings. Through this circular process of being responded to, the infant develops a sense of body and of self, as well as an aware-ness of 'other', and begins to experience people and objects outside the self as in her control.

When this process of need and response goes reason-ably well, the infant takes in biologically nourishing food as well as the psychologically nourishing experience of feeling emotionally and physically nurtured and sup-ported. Gradually, the infant internalizes a place of comfort and safety and learns that she can impact the environment, which is experienced as reliable enough and provides a soothing and pleasurable response to hunger in the form of touch and food. As long as the infant hasn't had to get too frantic or furious from being left alone too long when hungry or in other states of discomfort, she will develop good feelings about herself along with the ability to soothe and ultimately to feed herself.

When, for a variety of reasons ranging from the 'fit' between mother and baby to mother's own history of being mothered, this process goes less than smoothly, the baby's body and psychological self-development can be adversely affected. Then the feelings experienced by the frantic and often furious infant become concretized later in life and are given words: 'I am a bad (or ugly, or horrible) person'.

Other factors

Although we have emphasized the developing infant's relationship with mother, both parents or parent figures influence the culture in the family where body shape and food are concerned. Both parents may project their own anxieties about size and sexuality, about restraint and excess, on to their children. These anxieties can be compounded in families where there is a history of alcohol or drug abuse and/or physical or sexual abuse.

In our experience a client who is working through early traumas, such as rape, battering, or incest, may temporarily develop an eating disorder as a way of coping with powerful feelings of being victimized. These clients who are struggling with the reality of having been powerless may find some semblance of power in their ability to control what they eat.

Other life events that can trigger the onset of an eating problem or disorder are leaving home, the break-up of a relationship, starting a relationship, becoming a parent (or step-parent), and being bereaved. One way of coping with anxiety and stress is to eat. Most of us have some favourite or 'comfort' food. In western culture, with its idealizing of thinness, both girls and boys quickly learn that people who have bodies that deviate from the norm are valued less than others. Thinness becomes equated with perfection and control and is, often at the most profound level, inseparable from feeling good about one's self. The problem is that society also encourages excess, particularly seasonal excess. December's Sunday colour supplements are full of rich recipes for Christmas. January's will be full of diets and detox regimes.

Common factors in eating disorders

Disordered relationships with food are made even more complicated than disordered relationship with other substances, experiences, or people because we have to eat in order to live. Some of us even live to eat. It may be difficult to give up cigarettes and alcohol but there are acceptable substitutes and alternative experiences. There is no substitute for food. Eating problems are made even more complicated because food is symbolic of so much for us – love, status, pleasure, sex.

Bulimia, anorexia, and compulsive eating may appear different; however, they all share a preoccupation with eating, food, weight, body fat, and body-image. The relationship with food has become a reliable substitute for more complex human relationships. Underlying all three are issues of feeling invisible and difficulties with separation, dependence/independence, and control. Therapists working with eating disorders need to be aware that the disordered behaviours will more than likely increase across the range of eating disorders as clients are helped to be more in touch with their feelings.

The therapist also needs to understand that clients in the grip of anorexic behaviour and its associated thinking are not available to take in *anything* and will not be able to benefit from relational or insight-oriented therapies. Clients with bulimia are more available between binges to look at the underlying causes of their behaviour, as are compulsive overeaters. Having said that, the therapist working with clients with eating disorders needs to be able to work closely with the transference–countertransference dynamic, particularly in the early stages of therapy when the client will not have words to describe her feelings and will not be able to take in the therapist's words. Farrell (2000) describes these clients as 'lost for words'.

Transference and countertransference

How each of us chooses what, when, and how much we eat can be a metaphor for how we live our lives; how much of life and people we take in. The process is mirrored in the relationship between therapist and client. Helping eating disordered clients have a nourishing and varied relationship with us helps them to have better relationships with their bodies and sensations, with their emotions, and with others. That's the theory in a nutshell. In practice it can be hellishly difficult for both the client and the therapist.

As we have said, people with eating disorders invariably feel alienated and isolated and struggle painfully in their relationships with self and others. The therapeutic relationship will be no exception. It becomes a boundaried space, like a stage, where external and internal relationships can be recreated, often with all the attendant drama and suspense.

Holding, containing, and working with our emotional resonance or with what is projected on to us by clients suffering from eating disorders can be challenging indeed. The client brings her inner landscape with her and recreates it in the consulting room. The therapist will, at the very least, be seen as allying with the persecuting, perfection-demanding culture, or as a judge who will think the client is weak, pathetic, disgusting, useless, fat, unlovable, and generally undeserving of good things in life. The therapist will also at times be seen as a potential 'saviour'; a perfect human being who has escaped the restrictions of ordinary human frailty and who has the key to her happiness, however much she may accuse you of not making her better!

It is often very difficult for a therapist not to start behaving – or at least to be tempted to behave – like a judge or like a saviour. We must remember that, among other things, the client projects a rescuing or withholding saviour and judge on to the therapist in order not to relive painful childhood feelings through actually doing the work. The client has come into therapy believing that there is a *right* way to be and is waiting for you to show it to her, just like she waited and waited for mother to mobilize her and, thus, to set her free.

Because these clients often had controlling or invasive mothers, the therapist's mind and body are under very close scrutiny by clients with eating disorders and this can feel very exposing. It can often feel as if the client needs to use the therapist's body until she discovers more about her own. Clients who have not been attuned to as children will be exquisitely attuned to the therapist's non-verbal communication, scrutinizing every word and gesture in an attempt to protect themselves from the hostility they have come to expect from important others.

A colleague equates these clients to drowning swimmers who, in their frantic desperation to stay afloat, pull the life-guard down with them. The therapist's attempts to 'save' the client with empathy and holding are actively fought against because of the extent to which people with body-image and eating problems experience existential self-loathing.

In the struggle to stay afloat the therapist's own sore spots will be, at the very least, bruised. The therapist's responses can range from feeling redundant, guilty, disorganized, and furious to feeling emotionally and physically drained and dreading the sessions, or to overeating or drinking in order to fill the emptiness. Although these responses come from a place inside the therapist, they also need to be understood as communications from the client about her feeling-states and relational experiences. We have come to believe that managing, understanding, and using our emotional resonance is the most potent tool the therapist has for 'knowing' the inner world of the client as well as how other people in the client's life have treated them. And we have learned, at our cost, the need to anticipate our responses to certain clients as well as to anticipate our need to seek support and other means of processing and protection.

How to recognise eating disorders

Given that complicated relationships with food are commonplace, how do we know when a complicated

116

relationship or tendency becomes a serious problem? When working with people with eating disorders the therapist needs to be aware of the assumptions she may make about food and size. Not all overweight people are compulsive/obsessive eaters. Neither are all very thin people anorexic. It is critical not to assume that weight is a problem for the client. It may just be a problem for the therapist. Having said that the following 'signs' may be of use to you.

- Many people depend on rigid food control and exercise routines for a sense of 'self'. Although these people may not show obvious physical symptoms, they are often vulnerable to developing serious eating problems. Those most at risk are those clients who lead narrow, predictable, and colourless lives. These clients may report hoarding things such as money, stamps, plastic bags, newspapers, or food and water in case of national disaster.
- Some clients place a very high emphasis on perfectionism. In our experience, clients who refer to themselves as 'pathetic' or 'stupid' or 'useless' might also be women who secretly berate themselves for being unable to control what they eat.
- Clients who find it difficult or seem to be unable to be assertive and to say 'no' and to know what they want may also be living with someone who requires them to look a certain way or even to eat to please them.
- Listen out for statements a client makes that may indicate a core belief that what they eat is who they are. These people may, often apparently jokingly, call themselves bad or naughty and often begin a session

by giving the therapist an update on the previous week or weekend. Reporting that they had a 'good week' is often code for having not binged.

- Obviously underweight clients who talk about rising early and going to the gym before work might be hiding hunger-induced sleeplessness and be using excessive exercise to control their weight.
- Bulimic clients are the most difficult to identify when they don't present with problems with food, as their behaviours are by necessity hidden. Clients with chronic bulimia will have some physical signs in the form of teeth that have been capped to hide the deterioration of the enamel caused by constant stomach acid interacting with the teeth and they may have excessive, peach-fuzzy facial hair and 'chipmunk-like' cheeks. Perfume and breath spray may be used excessively to disguise the signs of having recently vomited.

Therapeutic attitude

Anyone who has ever fed and changed a baby or who has ever tried to get a child to eat something it doesn't like knows that feeding can be a messy business. Just as food can be chewed up and swallowed or spat out, sicked-up or excreted so can even most well-informed and intended interventions.

The therapist's own needs for order, control, and to make sense out of chaos will be triggered when working with clients with eating disorders. Staying with the 'mess' these clients bring is an essential part of the work.

Our attitudes towards messiness must be explored in therapy and supervision. Therapists working with clients with eating disorders need to ask themselves how they feel about: vomiting and making oneself sick by sticking various things down one's throat; taking laxatives; regurgitating – keeping food in the mouth by swallowing and bringing it back up; storing vomit in bags under the bed; hoarding and stealing food; cutting or burning the body with cigarettes; pulling out hair; using kitchen disinfectants, shampoo, or washing-up liquid to clean out one's system. Although we may feel repulsed by some of these behaviours it is also possible to become fascinated in a voyeuristic way.

We once worked with a family. The mother was a committed anorexic who also employed bulimic behaviours to keep her weight down. When we first met her she had no hair and looked like Munch's *The Scream*. She had been at death's door more times than her husband could remember. They had three children. In order to make the children think she was following doctor's orders and eating, she would share an evening meal with the family and then drink washing-up liquid to make sure she got rid of 'all of it'. I once had to leave the room in the middle of a session because I thought I might be sick. Outside of sessions we talked about this woman more than was good for us, and realized that we were secretly fascinated with how she managed to do all these terrible things to herself and still be alive at fifty-two.

Clients with eating disorders are super-sensitive to the attitudes of others, constantly looking to the therapist for confirmation of their own demand for self-perfection on the one hand and self-loathing on the other. We need to examine our own relationships with food and our bodies and how we manage and think about our own and others' weight and size. It is possible that the therapist will feel superior to clients who are overweight or can only control their weight by resorting to drastic measures. Do we feel self-righteous that we are within accepted social norms for body size or are we ashamed that we are not? Do we admire hard work, perfectionism, and will power? Do we know our own compulsive potential? Can we accept our own greed?

Working with obese clients

As we have said, not all overweight or obese clients are people who compulsively eat. Genetics, metabolism, levels of activity, and hormone levels all affect the extent to which food gets used as energy or is turned into fat.

Whatever the causes, current research indicates that obese people with mainly abdominal, 'apple-shaped', distribution of fat are more at risk of developing cardio-vascular disease and type II diabetes than are those with more general, 'pear-shaped', fat distribution. Obesity-related illness now accounts for health costs of about £2 billion annually in the UK.

Compulsive eaters tend to interpret their emotional hunger as physiological hunger. Food acts as a way of soothing the anxious and distressed feelings that result from the lack of an internalized soothing other.

What is often not recognized by the compulsive eater, who in a rather concrete way believes that all her problems would be solved if she were thin, is that she is very frightened of being thin. Thin can mean feeling too powerful, sexual, or competitive. Just as thinness is feared so is the possibility of starving that comes to light when a compulsive eater contemplates reducing her intake of food. This fear represents her fear of emotionally starving; of exposing her needs and having them remain unmet. There is often warmth and comfort in being big, but this is often difficult for her to acknowledge. Weight can also be used to defend against a childhood trauma, such as neglect or sexual abuse.

Fiona was in her mid-forties when she came into therapy because she had gained something like six stone in the ten years since her twin sister's death. She was a very large woman who moved with grace and elegance despite her size. She told her therapist, half-jokingly, that she believed she was possessed by a demon. She said, laughing, 'I don't know why I eat so much. The devil makes me do it!'

This language suggesting demonic possession alerted the therapist to avoid colluding with Fiona's feelings of being in any way unacceptable and the therapist deftly avoided ever directly working with the issue of whether or not she needed to lose weight. By refusing to take up the client's invitation to agree that she was 'the bad one in the family', the therapist set the stage for Fiona to explore her feelings, held since childhood, that she was the bad twin. Fiona was the second-born and mother, who was in her forties, never really recovered from the birth. She would often say that she would have been all right if she'd only had one baby. Nevertheless, Fiona was fiercely protective of mother and the therapist always respected this, although she held in her mind that Fiona might be sacrificing herself to being fat in order to atone for the 'sin' of making mother ill.

She once brought into the session a card she had made for her mother in infant school that she had found in a drawer in her mother's house. The children had been asked to write stories and the teacher typed them up to go inside the card with the child's drawing on the outside. Five-year-old Fiona had just scribbled on the outside with red and black crayon – there were no discernible shapes, just 'angry' marks. The story went as follows: 'There once was a little girl who went to the circus. On the way she met a wolf. She screamed and stabbed a knife at the wolf. Then a little boy came and the mother said 'Come home this instant'. Then the little girl said, 'I'm coming home at 100 minutes after 11. Then she pushed her house down, ate everything inside of it and then she was dead.'

Fiona's story, written for her mother, shows a little girl who is raging at a controlling and uncaring mother and who turns her rage against herself by putting things into her mouth and 'deadening' herself. Although Fiona had no memories of ever feeling angry as a child this tells a different story.

The therapist diligently held on to her position of neutrality where Fiona's weight was concerned. When she would report that she'd been eating all weekend the therapist would respond with genuine interest in what else had been going on at the time. When, after two years of therapy and a six-week summer break, Fiona arrived having lost a considerable amount of weight, the therapist suppressed a desire to comment on how good she looked and, rather, focused on how glad she was to see her again after so many weeks. Even when Fiona would, apparently deliberately, try to put the therapist off by relating stories of excessive and often gross nocturnal binging, the therapist would respond with a normalizing intervention ('night time is a time when many women turn to food for company') as well as with empathy ('knowing you as I do I imagine you were feeling lonely yet were ashamed to pick up the phone and leave a message on my answering machine').

Gradually, Fiona was able to feel genuinely respected by her therapist and secure enough in the relationship so that she could be angry with the therapist for having double-booked an appointment (remember Fiona was a twin!). The therapist was able to show Fiona that she could survive her anger, in fact, that she welcomed it because it was genuine. After several weeks Fiona came to realize how she had given her sister all the goodness in their world and had blamed herself for not being mother's favourite.

Four years into the therapy Fiona is probably three stone lighter than she was when she began. She has taken up cycling and line dancing and, although she still occasionally binges, she accepts these incidents as part of who she is and as signals that she needs to attend more to her self-care. She has decided to exclude wheat and dairy products from her diet and in that way imposes 'limits' on what she eats. Despite the restrictions her new ways of eating impose on her she says that she feels free for the first time in her life.

Therapists, particularly those who have never battled with their weight or who have never used food (or other things) as a substitute for human warmth, may find it difficult to resist supporting an overweight client to diet as a way of increasing their self-esteem. In so doing, inadvertently they are asking the client to end the most consistent and exciting relationship in their life without having any with which to replace it. Only once Fiona was able to replace her need for food with internal images of her relationship with her therapist could she begin to alter her relationship with food. That relationship has changed and

Fiona has lost weight but, most importantly for her, she accepts herself as she is and treats her still large body with increasing respect, if not love.

The bulimic client

The term *bulimia nervosa* was first used by Russell in 1979 to describe clients who suffer from powerful and intractable urges to overeat while maintaining normal body weight. A bulimic often feels like a failed anorexic because she 'gives in' to the demands of hunger. Feelings of depression are very much part of her inner life. She is caught in a – usually daily (often many times a day) – cycle of bingeing and purging that is often interspersed with periods of starvation and can lead to serious loss of potassium, the erosion of teeth enamel, and enlargement of the salivary glands. There is also a risk of osteoporosis. People who engage in bulimic behaviours of bingeing and then purging, either by vomiting or by taking laxatives, are at risk of cardiac arrest due to the electrolyte imbalance that is created by their behaviours.

Bulimia is more difficult to recognize than obesity or anorexia because bulimics are usually of normal weight and their behaviours are often hidden in the privacy of their home – particularly in the bathroom. Bulimia can also be masked by another behaviour. I once worked with a woman who came to work on drinking less. Years later, through a colleague that she consulted after she finished with me, I discovered she was bulimic.

People who engage in bulimic behaviours suffer from depressed and angry moods, and have extremely self-attacking thoughts. They are often over-achievers in the work-place and any other area of their lives where they demand perfection of themselves and others. They respond to their 'imperfection' by metaphorically whipping themselves with self-disgust. They hide their feelings of being needy and out-of-control, which are manifest in the bulimic cycle.

Bulimic clients tend to believe that by controlling what goes in and out of their body they can master what feels uncontrollable, even unnameable. They relocate their distress or trauma – injuries of neglect, exploitation, deprivation, homophobia, racism – in their bodies

Bulimia can also be understood as a way of coping with the real and imagined demands of having to negotiate a rapidly shifting social world. This may be why bulimia is so much more common in women than in men. We have noticed that our bulimic clients often describe their families as not having enough room – often literally – for them, or as not being interested in their achievements.

Normal weight bulimic women were usually 'good' girls who did not make demands but from whom much was expected. They tend to come from families where anger, assertion, or rebellion went underground. Inside them is a raging child who is still clamouring for attention. Many of our clients are linked by having had a family member with a serious illness or a physical or emotional problem that took up a lot of space. As children, their needs went underground. As adults, on the surface they seem to drive themselves to be the best they can be while projecting their needy self on to the food that they then expel down the toilet as unacceptable. The bathroom becomes the secret lair of the bulimic, a room of her own where she can be alone with the chaos and despair that she hides from everyone else.

Bulimic clients binge in secret, fearing, on the one hand, that others will want to take the food away and, on the other hand, feeling so ashamed of their behaviour and the neediness it represents that they need to hide from others. Even the act of buying food can be threatening to some bulimics as it shows that they are 'needy'. So they steal it.

If food represents love/need, then eating can represent an attempt to get some good mothering at last. Food is seductive, promising, but never provides nurture and acceptance. Once taken in, the feelings that are kept at bay when not eating begin to invade and the bulimic feels taken over by discomfort and chaos. These feelings turn quickly into self-hate. She feels grotesque and out of control, full of profound shame and self-disgust. Purging, usually through vomiting, becomes the solution to ridding herself of these intolerable feelings. Purging gives her the illusion that she can do something about her self-loathing. It helps her to re-establish her boundaries and to get rid of the invader. She feels better, peaceful. One client described a 'perfect state of numbness'. This 'perfect state' soon passes and the thought occurs that eating is the answer to the discomfort of feeling empty/hungry/unloved. And the cycle begins all over again.

It is the feeling states that accompany the completion of the binge that account for the addictive aspect of bulimic behaviour. In the previous chapter we looked at how people become addicted to an experience more than to the substance itself. Euphoria is addictive. And it is worth going through the more unpleasant aspects of the cycle to achieve it. The therapist needs to take seriously just how good the client feels doing something that may sound repulsive to the therapist.

Through binging and purging the bulimic is symbolically recreating her experience of not having enough and of what she did have (mother's food/love) being somehow toxic. This process is costly at many levels. It takes a toll on one's health and eats away at the body. And bulimics who live away from home and have to pay for their own food are always short of money

Helen

Helen is a young woman in her twenties who came into therapy because she felt she was going out of control with her bulimic behaviour. She wanted to break the cycle of secrecy and deceit that she had been caught up in since her teens.

She saw herself as 'disgusting'. She couldn't bear to look at her body and worried continuously about what she imagined others felt about her appearance. (Her therapist saw her as attractive and of normal weight.) She felt guilty for being and she felt guilty for eating. As is so often true of women with eating disorders, she felt a deep conviction that there was something wrong with her. Her fear of causing pain to others drove her to take on more and more work until she couldn't cope and began to feel 'pushed over the edge'. She was bingeing and vomiting several times a day in order to relieve her distress. Following a binge she would attack herself for being weak, stupid, and incompetent because she 'wasn't coping'. Binging and purging had become a frantic search for emotional warmth and comfort when she felt 'stressed out' or neglected, as well as the means of punishing herself for what she perceived were her imperfections.

Helen described her boyfriend as like a 'personal trainer', forcing her to exercise in the gym, watching her closely while eating, and continually criticizing her. The therapist was alerted to the possibility that she would have critical feelings towards Helen, who made very little eye contact and sat in the chair as if to take up the smallest amount of space possible. She appeared young and very unsure of herself. She talked fast, stumbling over some words, mumbling others, and the therapist had great difficulty in understanding what she was saying. She tended to race through any story until she reached the point of self-blame as this was where her energy was focused and what, if anything, she seemed particularly to enjoy.

The therapist started to wonder if Helen was, perhaps, through her mumbling and speed and self-blame, inviting her not to really listen and take her seriously, as Helen would regularly complain that no one in her life *had* taken her seriously. Her first task was to slow her down and to support her to give a fuller, step-by-step account of her journey into binging and purging, and to describe her experience of hating her body and her self while making a bit more contact.

Helen's feelings towards her therapist changed from session to session. At times she saw the therapist as someone, like her mother, who had to be protected from her anger. She could easily imagine her as critical, and as demanding that she be more 'perfect', i.e. physically thinner and emotionally less needy. At other times she saw the therapist as she saw her grandmother, as warm and accepting and as a supportive, positive influence in her life.

The therapist experienced many conflicting and, at times, troubling, responses to Helen. Initially, she felt maternal and protective – wanting to take care of her and 'rescue' her from the 'attackers' in her life – starting with the vicious one inside her. She has felt empty, tired, ungenerous, and hard, particularly when holding the boundary at the end of the session. The therapist found that her initial feelings of warmth soon turned to anxiety at trying to keep up with Helen's pace. The anxiety soon turned to frustration and then to exhaustion. Eventually, she noticed that she had given up listening to her altogether. She realized that she had colluded with the client's expectation of not being important enough. Once she became aware of how she was subtly enacting her countertransference she was able to monitor this process between them.

She also had to watch for how, at times, she tended to work very hard in order to hear and understand and be with someone who made all these things pretty difficult. It was easy to become drained and therefore more vulnerable to becoming a persecutory, attacking 'other'. She decided to change Helen's end-of-week, late afternoon appointment to a morning one earlier in the week, when she tended to be more resourced.

The therapist realized this work was going to be difficult, even though on the surface Helen seemed very invested in 'getting well'. Helen was unaware of the part of her that was rigid in her self-hatred, believed she was 'bad', and seemed to fear having anything good. (Remember that taking precedes giving.) The part of Helen that was invested in destroying anything positive that might be offered to her would very likely work to destroy the benefits of psychotherapy. Helen's parents had an emotionally volatile relationship, and she saw her mother as a verbally aggressive woman who frequently vented her anger and rage by criticizing Helen and regularly comparing her unfavourably with other girls. As a result Helen had great difficulty with anger and aggression. Unable to own her own, she saw it only in others. If she felt unhappy about someone's behaviour towards her, her fear of hurting them and her fear of their anger prevented her from saying anything.

The therapist was aware that Helen's bulimic behaviour would probably get worse in the early stages of therapy as Helen struggled with her emotional conflicts in relationship with another who could accept her even when she 'failed'. Not only did Helen report that her bingeing and purging was 'out of control', she also reproduced it in the therapy sessions, seeming on the one hand starving for reassurance and warmth then spitting it back at the therapist in cascades of self-attack.

Over a period of five years Helen eventually came to see that she felt angry and attacking towards significant others in her life for abandoning her, and that she had turned that anger against herself. She also came to realize that her mother had envied her for being active and demanding the way all infants naturally are. She further realized that she would engage in bulimic behaviour to punish herself for having fun and for achieving things in her career and in therapy. It was a challenge for her therapist to not take as a sign of defeat that Helen would report having binged just when she seemed to be getting better. Her therapist had to pay close attention to controlling her urge to criticize – even reject – her client, which she came to understand as a defence against her own feelings of failure. By understanding that the feelings that were being evoked in her were a part of the bulimic process she could remain a benign 'other' in the face of her client's attempts to attack herself and the therapy.

She was also able to 'interpret' the process for Helen by saying, 'When you feel good here you may fear that I will feel envious, so you attack yourself before I can attack you.' Helen is now managing to endure the discomfort of feeling good following a therapy session without resorting to bingeing and purging. She now runs to help manage her inner tension, but does this increasingly for pleasure, not punishment.

Helen is now able to keep eye contact with her therapist for extended periods and allows herself to feel 'fed' by her therapist's face. In her close relationships, she experienced a pattern of gradually coming to feel attacked and mistreated as the relationship progressed. She believed that this was because she fell short of their expectations. After five years in therapy she now has a relationship where she feels safe to be herself. She experiences her therapist as someone who is not threatened by her success or crushed by her 'failures'. The conflicts that were initially located in 'the other', are increasingly being re-owned and survived in the presence of an 'other' who can just 'let me be me'.

Helen is now at a place in her journey where she can see that it is *she* who is unhappy with her boyfriend and not the other way around. She is also able to understand the 'danger' of allowing herself to accept that other men might be attracted to her and that entering into the process of starting a new relationship could trigger her bulimic behaviour. She has decided to 'see what happens'; to see less of her current boyfriend while exploring the dynamics of that relationship in therapy.

Guidelines for treatment of bulimic clients

1. Build up the therapeutic alliance by attending to the client as closely as she can tolerate; listen, attune, and accept.

2. Remember that the client has been 'injured' in the process of taking and giving and that she will find it difficult to take from the therapist. She will also find it difficult to give, and this will be evident in the therapist's feeling of depletion.

3. Take the symptoms seriously. Acknowledge them as an indication of a part of the client that wants to be heard, even though client and therapist may not yet understand what is being said. Help the client to trust that the words behind the symptoms are inside her, probably have their roots in her childhood experience, and will become clearer over time.

4. Slow the client down, i.e., 'I am curious about how much I really want to know and understand you, yet I'm beginning to wonder if your "speediness" is telling us something about how you feel about anyone being curious about you.'

5. Help her to become aware of her apparent need to focus on her negative self-perceptions and to be curious about origin and function of this attack on the self.

6. Help the client to 'retrace her steps' to see what triggers her into the bingeing. In order not to trigger self-attack do not focus on the behaviour alone, but support the client towards identifying how her behaviour hides powerful feelings towards self and others that she has held since her childhood.

7. Slowly and carefully track the client's process on each step of the journey that begins with reaching for food and ends with self-recrimination after having vomited; therapist and client will have to repeat this process again and again.

8. Meet the client's developmental need to be understood, mirrored, and heard in order to challenge the

self-hatred that is particularly evoked when the client feels needy.

9. Help the client to see the 'adaptive' function of the bingeing and purging.

10. Expect and get regular help to manage intense countertransference responses to the client, her behaviour, and to the people in her life who have hurt her. Be vigilant in order not to join the long list of people who criticize her and/or fail her.

11. The process of the relationship with the therapist needs to be continually addressed in order for the client to re-experience the longing for merger and her rage.

Anorexia

The diagnosis of anorexia nervosa has been with us since the nineteenth century. Early theories (Freud 1931; Lasègue, 1873) stressed a conflict about sexuality as being at the root of the problem as amenorrhea is common and normal 'female' development (breasts, pubic hair) is stunted. In our experience, people with anorexia have taken the solution to their hunger for food/love not being met by appearing to be completely free of need. Emptiness has become an ideal.

Anorexics are obviously thin people who see themselves as fat, even though they may understand that *you* and others see them as alarmingly thin. The psychotropic effects of starvation take hold very quickly – in fact, only a few hours without food creates a sense of euphoria. Continued starvation disrupts the thinking processes as the euphoria becomes addictive. When a person decides to continue to starve herself she is not in the same physical and psychological state as when the initial decision not to eat was made. The therapist needs to watch for the changes in personality in clients who appear to rapidly lose weight. These changes are driven by starvation, and the client will need to be referred to a specialist. The endorphins released by starvation act quickly, and the client's ability to think will be affected. This will be reflected in their belief that they are too fat or that they don't need to eat. Anorexia has the highest death rate of all psychiatric disorders. Clients with anorexia who are not able to maintain a reasonable body weight are in grave danger and should never be seen by a therapist, no matter how experienced, who is not in contact with an adjunct professional (see Onward Referral, below).

An anorexic is always hungry, yet is preoccupied with not eating and surviving each day. She is rigidly committed to having will-power, being rational, controlled, and projecting an 'I feel fine' persona. Her sense of self is so dependent on her controlling her food that if she loses this control she fears feeling annihilated. This is important to remember, because if we support the client's blossoming desire to change her behaviours before she has enough internal and external support to do so, the client's very life may be endangered. At the very least a client who stops starving herself may go through a sort of 'cold turkey' reaction and may also experience intense physical pain.

An anorexic does not feel depressed because she keeps feelings away by starving herself and producing the associated euphoric feelings. She also feels proud of the rigid discipline and self-control that it takes not to eat, and this increases her self-esteem. Feelings of depression and panic will emerge when she begins to gain weight and may trigger the client back into the starvation cycle.

It is important, also, to remember that an anorexic's emotional development will have been slowed down, even arrested, at the point of onset of the disorder. We are generally working with someone who is on the one hand emotionally very young and who, on the other hand, has lost years of youth to the rigid demands of this illness.

Anorexics can be of the restrictive type, described above, or can have a more complex presentation that involves purging in order to remain underweight and of using alcohol, drugs, and laxatives to avoid weight gain. Both types share a grossly distorted perception of themselves as being fat, when in fact they are alarmingly – often life-threateningly – thin.

The examples given below are from our work with anorexic clients whose body weight is stable and who are or have been supported by adjunct professionals. They were no longer considered 'at risk' of dying from the effects of starvation when they entered therapy. If you suspect that a client is anorexic you must abandon any introjects you may have about allowing the client to be an equal partner in the therapy and may need to be brutal in insisting that your client seek specialist advice from a psychiatrist and/or a nutritionist before agreeing to work with her.

Carolyn was in her late twenties when she presented for psychotherapy. She had been anorexic since her mid-teens. She was a restrictive-type anorexic who had received out-patient psychiatric treatment and her weight was stable at 6½ stone. Her periods had stopped years ago. She complained of aching limbs whenever she put on a few pounds. Through an iron will she continued to work as a waitress six days a week, feeding others while starving herself. Carolyn got up very early in order to run several miles a day before going to work. She also went to an enormous amount of effort to prepare and cook meals for others socially. She tended to live on salads. If she ate a proper meal in the evening then she would go for a longer run the next morning.

Carolyn was totally unforgiving of herself whenever she, in her mind, had fallen short of her goal of perfection. Carolyn's inner landscape was bleak and the cruelty in the tone of voice she used towards herself made the therapist wince in pain on more than one occasion. Being with Carolyn was like being with someone who relentlessly whipped herself. When she wasn't tearing herself apart verbally, and attacking her body through exercise and self-denial she imagined that others in her life were being deliberately 'horrid' towards her.

The therapist was frequently experienced as the perpetrator of punishment and persecution. The problem for both anorexics and bulimics is how to make a link with another person who can be allowed to be good.

Carolyn frequently missed sessions. Her therapist was able to connect this to Carolyn's early experience of being fed every four hours. She never challenged Carolyn's missing sessions but, rather, connected this to Carolyn's need to be in control of the feeding process. She let her know that she would be there for her whether she attended or not. Knowing this made Carolyn feel that the therapist was there for her in a way her mother was not when she was a child. She recently said to her therapist, 'I once had to fight you for control. Now I feel safe here most of the time.' Interestingly, now that Carolyn feels held in therapy she reports being less rigid in her life and is far less hard on herself.

Woodman (1982) describes eating disorders as 'addiction to perfection', McDougall (1989) believes that all forms of addiction serve to repair a damaged self-image that invariably includes an attempt to settle accounts with the introjected parents. The unconscious message to the internalized mother is 'You can never again abandon me. From now on *I* control *you!*'

To the internalized – and usually absent – father the message is, 'You weren't around for me and I don't give a shit what you think about me and how I lead my life. You can go to hell!'

The addictive solution to psychic pain seeks to repair a damaged self while maintaining the illusion of omnipotent control. The message to the world and to the therapist is, 'Nothing can touch me' and, in more desperate conditions: 'Maybe I will die from doing this. Who cares?'

Feeling 'invisible', the anorexic gives shape and substance to her inner emptiness. She believes that love and connection mean danger. Mothers of women like this in some way want their daughters to be extensions of them and feel rage when the child emerges as a separate, lively person. This rage is usually repressed and is expressed as control. The child feels so defective and under attack or held back that she splits off a part of herself that is, in her mind, hers and hers alone. Mothers of anorexics are manipulative and invasive. One client had a mother who used to say goodnight to her every night by pointing 'loudly' at her own cheek and saying to her child, '*Now* who do you love best – mummy or nanny?'

Another, Ruth, who was slightly chubby as a child, was taken from one doctor to another by a mother who was desperate to have a thinner daughter. When she naturally lost the weight as she moved into adolescence, her mother started on other aspects of her appearance; her hair was too thin, her feet too flat. This client remembers being taken to a gynaecologist for a pelvic examination at the age of fourteen and thinking, 'I will not let anyone control me' while at the same time feeling overwhelmingly impotent. She began that evening to diet obsessively. Control over her own body became her life's goal.

Soon she began to experience completely new feelings. She felt powerful – triumphant – even. Her weight dropped by two stone in six months and her periods soon stopped. She believes that her mother was threatened by her thinness as all the visits to doctors stopped once she became obviously, dangerously thin. Father, she said, didn't seem to notice.

Ruth was lucky. When she was at university, where she made a relationship with a tutor by whom she felt respected and encouraged to 'shine' as an academic, she began to realize that she could never get skinny enough to change her envious mother and 'absent' father. She frightened herself with a fantasy that she might die physically but that she would haunt them forever. She began to eat again and soon reached 'normal' weight. Her periods started again but she rarely had sexual relationships. She said that in her twenties she was only able to have sex when she was drunk. She came into therapy when she was in her late thirties and eventually revealed that she had a 'secret' alcohol problem (see Chapter Four).

Multi-impulsive disorders

Some clients may present with an eating disorder, but may also be hiding some other serious, self-harming behaviour.

Typically, when one behaviour is under control these clients tend to take up another one. They are are notoriously difficult to treat as they seem to have a vast repertoire of substitute behaviours and can endlessly avoid their feelings.

Tessa presented with bulimia. It emerged that she had a history of sexual promiscuity, which she believed was 'under control'. Instead, she burnt her arm, breasts, and thighs with a cigarette, picking at the scabs until they became infected, leaving her covered in scars, which she attempted to hide under her clothes. She also pulled out hair from her head, arms, and legs when very distressed, and often controlled her weekend bingeing and purging by spending vast amounts of money on her credit cards, only to take the goods back to the shop the next day.

Tessa was often 'wordless', sitting in silence and expecting the therapist to fill these silences. Initially the therapist felt tender and protective of Tessa, noticing how much she wanted to ease this young woman's pain and despair about herself. Gradually, this turned to unease and fear as the client reported moving from one self-harming behaviour to another and as her weight gradually increased. Every change Tessa made in her life – going on holiday, moving house, joining a gym, socializing with friends – began with enthusiasm, but was inevitably followed by failure to achieve any lasting change and, ultimately blaming the therapist for her lack of success, ('This isn't working. I think I should try something else').

Tessa could not hold on to anything nourishing for herself for any length of time; any moments of closeness and feeling heard by the therapist were usually purged during the following session ('I don't know if I can afford to come any more'). As Tessa became increasingly paranoid and seemed to see everyone in her life – friends, strangers, and her therapist as judging and laughing at her, the therapist noticed that she too was feeling paranoid and despairing, even outside of the sessions.

In supervision, the therapist wondered if the strength of her identification with this client meant that Tessa's ability to relate in the real world was becoming impaired. In spite of having helped Tessa to feel and think through her cycles and to talk more about her process, she was unable to hold on to any of this between sessions, nor was she able to internalize the therapist as a positive figure in her inner world. Although her therapist was well aware that these forces against health and for the maintenance of the symptoms were to be expected when working with eating disorders, the multiple behaviours and the chronic nature of these symptoms alerted her to the possibility that Tessa might benefit from an in-patient, or disciplined out-patient eating disorder treatment, where she could be contained and held within a multi-disciplinary team.

The therapist's dilemma was that, if she referred Tessa, she would be confirming Tessa as a hopeless case. On the other hand, if she didn't refer her, she might not be taking this client's health-threatening behaviours seriously enough, nor the limitations of what could be achieved in once-a-week psychotherapy when Tessa was not only unable to moderate her symptoms but they were increasing.

Fortunately, as this client regularly brought up the possibility of looking for another therapist, her therapist was able to confirm Tessa's sense that she needed 'more' than was possible on a weekly basis, and to talk with her about the possibilities within the medical world. She also let her know that if she wanted to return, once her in-patient treatment was completed, this would of course be an option.

Onward referral

The above example highlights a genuine concern when working with clients whose dis-ease leads to a state of mental or physiological disease. Therapists need to consider in supervision the need to work in association with other professionals, such as a psychiatrist, the GP, or a dietician when the client's behaviour is posing a genuine health risk, and should let the client know at the beginning of the therapeutic relationship that it may be necessary to discuss the client's progress (or lack of it) with a medical professional. The therapist needs to put across that these consultations are for her professional support and not an indication of the client's illness. Ultimately, through consultation, onward referral may be seen as the only option, even where the client has not raised this as a possibility. In these instances the therapist needs to focus on the limits of her competence, at the same time accepting the client's experience of being 'abandoned' or 'exiled.'

CHAPTER SIX

ENVY

Pride, envy, gluttony, avarice, lust, anger, sloth – we used to call them the Seven Deadly Sins – now we call them personality disorder or, more kindly, fragile self-process.

Human beings have been telling stories in order to explain the darker side of living and loving since the beginning of recorded time. Take the creation story in Genesis, for example. God tells Adam and Eve who, let's face it, have pretty much everything they could want, not to eat of the fruit of the tree of the knowledge of good and evil. The serpent, who envies Adam and Eve, takes Eve aside and tempts her to have a go. Eve's pride (she thought she knew better than God) and her greed (what she had wasn't enough) led to shame and exile. Some of my clients with 'overdoing' problems go through this cycle, sometimes several times a day. I've had plenty to eat. I shouldn't have a cream cake. I could have just one. I hate myself for being weak. I must hide my weakness from others or they will reject me. Interestingly, the 'original sin' that the creation myth described was induced by a power *outside* of Eve. Sin is usually explained as a response to an external stimulus or is ascribed to something else. The milk spilt, the ball broke the window, the devil made me do it. In other words, the stimulus is in the environment, not in the self.

When I was a child I was taught the view that was held pretty consistently by the Roman Catholic Church that pride was the greatest sin of all as it was a sin directly

143

against God. As an adult I don't have much difficulty seeing the positive aspects of most of the Seven Deadly Sins. Pride, even when it leads to destruction, has an important defensive element. I puff myself up to protect myself from attack. I am greedy when I fear that I or my loved ones won't have enough of something. Lust leads to sexual passion, which can be both creative and destructive. Without anger women and other 'minorities' would not have achieved the rights we now have. Gluttony and sloth – my particular favourites – when not chronic can provide an important retreat from stress and responsibility. In other words most of the Seven Deadly Sins are directed at achieving some sort of goal. Only envy is purely destructive. 'Envy destroys the possibility of hope' (Klein, 1957).

Not only is envy the only one of the Seven Deadly Sins that is in its most raw expression purely destructive, it is also the only one that is a verb as well as a noun. It's not something you just have or feel – it's something you do to others or yourself. Its intention, however well hidden, is to spoil.

I guess that the reason that envy – a concept key to psychoanalytic psychotherapies – is not discussed in most humanistic trainings is that pure envy has no light side. Humanistic psychotherapies, with their emphasis on the self-actualizing tendency (Rogers, 1951), organismic self-regulation (Perls, Hefferline, & Goodman, 1951), and hierarchies of needs (Maslow, 1970) do not focus on the conflicts inherent in the duality of human experience but rather believe that clients who come to therapy are doing the best they can to become the best they can be. I'm sure that most psychotherapists, whatever their orientation, also expect that people come into therapy really wanting

144

to change something, or to feel better, or to understand themselves better. I have struggled greatly myself as a therapist when this doesn't happen and, in the days of my TA and gestalt training, was encouraged in supervision to see what I might be doing to 'get in the client's way'. This is good supervisory advice. Yet focusing exclusively on what the therapist is bringing to a client's lack of forward movement misses what may be going on at a deeper level.

In his book *The Tyranny of Malice*, Berke (1988) recounts 'The Story of the Envious Man and Him who was Envied'. There are two neighbours, one a happy man who always does good and an envious man who is steaming with resentment. As far as he's concerned the good man can do nothing right. If the good man says, 'Good morning', the envious man says, 'Don't good-morning me you sanctimonious swine! How come my roof leaks and yours doesn't?' Eventually the good man moves away, having had enough of his neighbour's hostility. Naturally, he succeeds in everything he does. News of his success reaches the envious man, who decides to pursue him and throw him down a well. He does this, but a benevolent spirit intervenes and also teaches him how to cure the king's daughter. The good man is saved from death and gets to marry the king's daughter. In time the king dies and the good man becomes king. He calls for the envious man who says, 'How come you're the king and I'm not? Go ahead, then. Have me killed.' The king replies, 'Not at all, old friend, I'm going to make you a very rich man.' The envious man replies, 'You vindictive bastard!'

So why does the envious man see the good man as a vindictive bastard for making him rich? One possibility is that the envious man is perfectly happy being 'poor' – in

145

every sense of the word and using his 'poverty' to take swipes at everyone else. Another is that, because he knows about envy first hand, he fears being rich because he will attract the envy of others. Now, if we substitute 'therapist' for 'king' and 'difficult client' for 'envious man', we can begin to see the relevance of the parable to psychotherapy. Perhaps some clients really are content enough with the way they are in the world and fear the 'disintegration' that on some felt level they know must be involved in changing. It is also possible that some clients, particularly ones who grew up with envious parents, genuinely fear the riches of psychological growth, as they have come to expect that good things will be taken away from them. A third possibility is that a client who has been denied or deprived of 'goodness' for most of his childhood will imagine that the therapist has 'the goodies' and may envy the therapist for having what he believes he can never have. This third possibility also includes the probability that the client will envy the therapist and will want to destroy, or at least soil, her 'gifts'.

Clients will, by nature of the therapeutic relationship and the reasons for entering into it, see us as possessing something they do not. At some level they believe they need us in order to fix something that they cannot fix on their own. They may see their therapist as possessing qualities that they believe they lack or they may simply believe we have the answers to their questions. A client coming to therapy is admitting that she needs help from a professional, which immediately puts her in the 'weaker' position, no matter how much the therapist believes in co-creation, horizontality, or any of the other euphemisms we use to gloss over the real and transferential power imbalance in the therapeutic relationship.

146

Melanie Klein was not the first to write about envy in the therapeutic encounter but she is the one who put envy on the map. Klein's paper, 'Envy and gratitude', was her attempt to explain what had come to be known as the 'negative therapeutic reaction'. In simple language it is the term used to describe people who come into and appear to engage in psychotherapy but do not improve.

Klein believed that our earliest experience of power is of the comfort of knowing that mother has good things like milk and a warm body in sharp contrast to being denied these good things no matter how much we want them. Baby feels inferior and impotent. Mother calls the shots. Klein believed that envy was innate in the baby rather than, as I see it, that it is one of the earliest relational phenomena that may indeed begin with the baby needing an outlet for its rage at not being able to have what it wants, when it wants it. This rage gets transformed into a spoiling destructiveness. I remember as a child wanting an ice cream so badly that I threw it on the ground once I finally got it because it was the wrong flavour.

Here's how Klein describes the process:

> The baby's first object of love and hate – his mother – is both desired and hated with all the intensity and strength that is characteristic of the early urges of the baby . . . When the baby is hungry and his desires are not gratified, or when he is feeling bodily pain or discomfort, then the whole situation suddenly alters. Hatred and aggressive feelings are aroused and become dominated by the impulses to destroy the very person who is the object of all his desires and who, in his mind, is linked up with everything he experiences – good and bad alike. [1937, p. 306]

Too often I hear Klein dismissed by humanistic therapists and wonder if they have ever read her work.
Although language that describes a baby as *wanting* to
destroy his mother does not sit easily with humanistic
sensibilities, we can probably recognize in ourselves or
have experienced with others the blinding urge to want
to hurt the one we love. Klein explored through her own
lens and the metaphor of the good and bad breast the
duality of experience that is now pretty much taken for
granted, even in humanistic circles. Love and hate co-
exist and psychological dysfunction is often a reflection of
our impaired ability to hold both in awareness concur-
rently.

Some of her colleagues thought she went too far in
telling only one side of the story. Apparently Winnicott
sat in the audience when the paper was first given at a
conference in Geneva in 1955 with his head in his hands,
muttering, 'Oh no. She can't do this.'

'*This*' referred to what he saw as Klein explaining a
baby's aggression and rage as arising from its inner world
as opposed to from its relationship with mother. It's worth
remembering something that Klein seemed to ignore,
which is that envious babies grow into envious adults.
And Winnicott (1945) held the position that mother and
child 'live an experience together' (p. 152). In other
words, the baby may well be frustrated, aggressive, and
attacking, but the mother's job is to humanize these
aggressive states by living through them with the baby.
We've already established that the baby feels inferior and
inadequate, but if the mother also feels inferior and inadequate – and what mother doesn't – she may project
aspects of her own aggression on to the baby. She may see
her baby as demanding, invasive, and greedy. The degree

of envy that a mother feels towards her baby is in proportion to the degree of inadequacy that she experiences.

Ruth (see Chapter Four) had a mother who quickly switched from breast to bottle-feeding and who enjoyed telling Ruth how she had felt like a brood mare and was constantly exhausted because – as she saw it – Ruth was insatiable. I wonder what Ruth's life might have been like had her mother been able to recognize *her* envy of her baby and to tolerate Ruth's energy and appetite for life.

Everything from Christian art to modern advertising supports the myth that mothers instinctively love their babies. In my experience of working with women who suffer from post-natal depression, across the board they lacked a way to safely express their un-motherly – and often fleetingly murderous – feelings towards their babies.

The difficulty in discussing envy and in recognizing it in our clients and ourselves is that it is *always* out of our awareness. I know immediately when I am jealous. I need help to recognize my envy. Without that glimmer of recognition I will project my envy out on to others or life. Even when my feelings of envy become more available to me I am likely to use a milder term – jealousy – to describe them. This is an important distinction. As I understand it, jealousy always involves a threesome. When I am jealous I seek exclusivity and don't want to share the one I love with any one or any thing. I can be jealous of my partner's relationship with a friend, or child, or with an animal, or a hobby. I once had a client whose husband bred dogs. She became concerned because she found herself fantasizing about the dogs dying in a fire. She realized that she was jealous of her husband's relationship with the dogs and that she wanted to have him all to herself. She didn't consider how her husband might feel about losing his dogs. In her fantasy he and she live happily ever after in a dog-free world. She failed to add into the equation that *she* had a hobby that often took her to the other side of the world.

I understood the above example as jealousy rather than envy or greed because envious people see or sense that someone has something that they lack. They also believe that they can't have that thing so they seek to destroy it. 'If I can't have it or do it or be it then no one else can either.' The envious person projects her sense of inferiority on to the other and then sees 'other' as being superior and with-holding. She then sets about attacking the what she projects on to 'other', destroying the good so that both feel depleted.

Greedy people want to have all the goodies and to enjoy them all by themselves. The primary process in greed is introjection, supported by a fear that others will want to take from you what you've got. Greed is anxious hunger. Envy is defensive starvation.

Just as an infant may feel – 'sense' is probably a better word – as though its mother is deliberately withholding goodness, so does the client, who begins to feel as though the therapist is deliberately withholding the one piece of information with which he would be healed. In the face of the real or imagined withholding of the longed-for nugget, all of the therapist's other offerings are spat out or otherwise destroyed.

Some years ago a colleague told me about a client of hers with whom she felt stuck. She described her client as a bitter woman who saw everyone else as having a better time than she did and who spent a good deal of the therapy hour complaining that no matter how much she did for other people she never had nice things happen to her. My colleague recounted her frustration that this woman – although she turned up faithfully every week – showed no improvement at all over the eighteen or so months she had been in therapy. If anything she was getting worse or, at least, her complaining was getting worse. One day this client brought her therapist a jar of homemade marmalade. I asked her if she'd eaten any and she said, 'No. You know, I had this strange feeling that it might make me sick. And I like marmalade.'

It turned out that her client hated marmalade, but made it every year for her friends and family.

In my experience people who hate marmalade *really* hate marmalade, to the point where, if they accidentally put some in their mouth, they would instinctively spit it out. This was a metaphor for what the client was doing with her therapist's interventions. She spat them out. We wondered together what her early life had been like and how she had come to be a person who, expecting that what comes from others will be tainted, learnt to spit out whatever came her way in order to protect herself from a kind of psychic poisoning.

Some time later my colleague reported having made considerable progress with this client from the time she began to play around with the process of 'spitting out' and found a way to raise it in the therapy. During one particularly challenging session she had an image of feeding a baby something it did not want to eat and she shared it with the client, who appeared not to hear or to be at all interested. The client arrived for the next session holding a photograph, which she handed to the therapist, showing a little girl sitting on a toilet with a look of abject terror on her face, eyes wide and her hands placed defensively in front of her mouth as if to say, 'No!!'. Visible in the corner of the photograph was another hand, her mother's, holding a spoon.

151

When the therapist enquired about the story behind the photo, her client told her that she had started thinking after the last session about an incident from her childhood that she remembered particularly well, possibly because it had been recorded for posterity. She went on to tell of a time when she had been ill and her mother tried to get her to take her tablets by mashing them up and putting them in a spoonful of strawberry jam.

'I wasn't having any', she said. 'I could see white flecks in the jam and I knew it wasn't jam at all and thought it must be poison.'

A lengthy battle ensued, mother finally thrusting the spoon into her child's mouth and the child responding by spitting the whole lot right back at her. The therapist responded, 'It was as though you were fighting for your life', and her client, for the first time in eighteen months, visibly softened and began to sob uncontrollably.

My colleague came to view her client as a child who was not able to differentiate between what was good and bad. If mother's medicine was poisonous than perhaps her love was laced with poison too. The client's habit of picking oranges, making marmalade, and giving it 'lovingly' to her friends and family (and therapist!) made bitter-sweet sense in this context. The deeply envious client is loath to take anything in, either because on some level they fear it will poison them, or because it would make them feel more inferior than they already feel.

Low self-esteem

Understanding the interpersonal aspects of envy has helped me enormously to understand and to work with what is generically known as low self-esteem. Ashwin, whose book *Cronos and His Children* (2000) (www. human-nature.com/ashwin/) explores envy and its clinical manifestations from a cultural, mythological, and psycho-analytic perspective, reminds us that envy, when it is chronic, 'sees' what it wants or needs but can not allow satisfaction. More intractably, she says, it attacks goodness within the self by destroying any memory of goodness, any experience of hope achieved, any movement towards creativity, growth or relationship.

When there are early ruptures in the mother–child relationship the child fails – as we saw in the above example – to be able to differentiate between what is good and what is bad. This lack of ability to differentiate is manifested in splitting, an ego function that we discussed in Chapter Two that divides others and self into two entirely separate parts. This can lead later in life to eating disorders, learning difficulties, and other syndromes that reflect an imbalance in the process of introjection and projection.

Envy in a family system can have damaging consequences throughout the life-cycle, but particularly during the years in which a child develops from being exclusively dependent on mother and father to exploring the world, others, and her own creativity. In our culture children are often told that something is 'for their own good'.

Ruth (see Chapter Four) remembers constantly being stopped from doing fun things by her mother who would tell her that someone was going to get hurt. Children tend to want to do what pleases their parents but some parents regularly focus on what *not* to do. Ruth's mother was critical of whatever she produced: her faeces when she was just a baby, her early attempts at drawing, her first friends

at school, her choice of career, and any prospective partner. Although Ruth was a talented story-teller and, later,
writer (she showed me some of her school compositions
written when she was only nine or ten), Ruth's mother put
her creativity down with crushing consistency. If Ruth
showed her something she had written mother would
focus on its inaccuracies, or would tell Ruth that she spent
too much time in a fantasy world. On Ruth's occasional
attempts to tell a story at the dinner table as a child and
even later in life, her mother would often put her down
by saying, 'Ruth has such a vivid imagination.'

It's not difficult to imagine the long-term effect these
subtle and not so subtle putdowns have on a child. The
other side of the picture is that the parent is also deprived
of taking pleasure in the child's vitality and creativity.

This can lead to what Rosenfeld (1971) refers to as a
'gang in the mind'. He writes about the self-attacking in
some clients as appearing highly organized, as if the therapist were dealing with a powerful gang dominated by a
leader who controls all the members of the gang to see
that they support one another in making the attacks on
the self as powerful and as destructive as possible. The
potential for anything good is dominated by an expectation of something bad that becomes so firmly entrenched
it's like the Mafia, with its fingers on all aspects of society.
You can't see it but you know it's there. Children of
envious parents learn to attack themselves in order to
protect themselves from the unbearable pain of being
attacked by the ones they most need to please. Ruth came
to believe that she drank in order to attack herself as she
had come to be expected to be attacked as a child: for
what she had done badly and, particularly, for what she
had done well.

The intrapsychic and interpersonal process of someone with low self-esteem goes something like this: good things only happen to other people; this is because I don't deserve good things; when good things happen to others that means there's less for me. I once worked with a woman called Saskia, who at forty had put a successful career on hold in order to have a baby. She came to see me when the child was 2½ because she was finding it difficult to pick up her career again and was also extremely anxious about leaving her daughter with the au pair or anyone else. Saskia was extremely unmotivated and self-critical and, although I liked her a lot and she was ever such a 'pleasant' woman, I came to understand how she was consumed by envy. She believed that all of the colleagues with whom she used to compete successfully for jobs had now surpassed her and were actively trying to keep her from getting back on the circuit. Now, on some level this was probably true, but, rather than spur her on to compete, Saskia saw others' success as 'proof' that she was a failure.

Because I *do* believe that the past shapes the present I made various attempts to help her to explore her past. She was very reluctant to do this and would interrupt any retelling of a childhood experience by suddenly saying, 'Oh God, I'm *so* pathetic', and looking at me sheepishly. One day she was telling me a story of an encounter with a male colleague on a freelance job she'd done. I remembered a story that she had once told me about her schooldays and I said, 'That reminds me of Simon Brockwood.'

At first Saskia seemed amazed and touched that I had remembered the name of a boy who used to bully her. Then she said, 'Is there a tape recorder in here?'

I said, 'You find it hard to believe that I could remember something that is important to you.'

She was silent for a while and then replied, 'It's *Brook-wood*, by the way.'

I felt flat and a bit humiliated, as I often did with Saskia when I offered her something that showed her that I had been attending to her. Her response to my intervention could be seen as a devaluation of my creativity by a client who was entrenched in the belief that the world wanted to deny her hers.

Victims of envy often feel helpless and impotent. Their attacks on self and others are a means of self-protection as well as deflating the other. I tend to see low self-esteem and self-criticism as envy retroflected or turned against the self. As envy is the most destructive experience it is the most shameful and the most defended against. To acknowledge envy is to acknowledge inferiority. People with low self-esteem nearly always somehow delight in the specialness of their inferiority. To be the worst is, paradoxically, to be the best. It is often easy to miss the narcissistic aspects of this process but it is there.

Clinical applications

Using the concept of envy as a lens you might find it useful to look for the subtle ways that some clients 'spoil' moments of being understood by the therapist. It is unpopular in humanistic circles to say this, but I'd like you to at least consider the possibility that clients who seem almost energetically stuck in hopelessness or self-loathing may be trying to feel powerful in the only way they know how, by making you fail at what *you're* supposed to be good at.

This can work both ways. Searles (1979) talks about his schizophrenic patients, who only began to improve when he acknowledged his own envy of their money, social status – even craziness. What might you envy about your clients? I once worked with a client who was a social worker who had had his GP sign him off for stress. The real reason was that he was depressed and couldn't get out of bed in the morning. We got precisely nowhere until I realized in supervision that I was deeply envious of his being able to be off work for weeks, stay in bed watching the telly, and still get paid for it. I was so envious that I had become unable to hear how hopeless this man felt in every aspect of his life. Once I identified my envy, I was able to take him seriously and to stay with the hopelessness that used to just irritate me and to tolerate my own hopelessness when, just as he made some progress in the therapy, he would attack it for not being good enough.

I was able to respond to his expressions of futility by simply stating each time 'You feel hopeless'. I responded to his attacks on his progress or on my interventions by saying things like ' You are afraid that someone will want to spoil your success so you get there first' or 'You find it hard to believe that I could be pleased for you'.

Later on in the work, once he was less consistently hopeless and/or self-attacking, I began to suggest possible explanations, based on what he had told me of his childhood, for how he got to be the kind of man he was. For example, his father was a coal miner and seemed to deeply envy his son's success at school and his desire to go to university. My client would reject these suggestions but I was gently persistent over time, being supported by my supervisor not to let this man's envious father attack my creativity. I used empathy sparingly, as I was helped to understand that empathy leads to insight and insight leads to the 'gang' being activated. In fact, when clients who were children of envious parents reach the stage in therapy where they gain insight into the interpersonal origin of their difficulties in life, they may leave therapy to protect their internalized parent(s) from the therapist. It is useful to pre-empt this by putting into words what they might be feeling so that it does not get enacted. At this point in the therapy interventions that show compassion for the offending parent may be useful. So will interventions that show that you recognize the client's potential to sabotage before they can enact it.

Defences

Envy, like shame, is often recognized through its defences and shame is part of the envious dance. Children are told: 'Don't show off', 'Don't blow your own trumpet', because unconsciously envious parents want to protect the kids from the envy of others. Shaming comments are just about always the results of envy. The whole point is to avoid feeling the shame about being envious by becoming the shamer.

Foster's (1972) anthropological analysis of envy put forward the view that Western society defends against acknowledging envy, not so much because it is unspeakable, but because it is an admission of inferiority. As a result, shame may be both the result of envy *and* a defence against it. Envy can also be viewed as a defence against shame. Shame also involves a sense of inferiority. It is, however unpleasant, perhaps more socially acceptable to feel shame and the freezing or intense exposure that accompany it than to attack and spoil.

Envy is not always but can be a component of competition and emulation. Competition, when not fully owned, is often expressed passive–aggressively through putdowns or bitchiness, but the person making the bitchy remark can usually be made to see its bitchy side. Emulation can also be tinged with envy but it is more passive, having the flavour of 'if you can't beat them, join them'.

I was once walking down the street in New York wearing a fur coat (it was the 1970s – OK?) and a woman walked up to me, looked me straight in the eye and said, 'I covet that coat.'

This had an entirely different feeling from the anonymous strangers who used to walk down the street scratching the sides of parked cars with a penknife. The woman was able to acknowledge desire and to accept 'deprivation'. 'I want it and I can't have it but I don't want to spoil it.'

Idealization is often a defence against envy. The problem is that the more the other is idealized the more envy will inevitably be aroused over time. Idealization can, then, lead to devaluation – if someone is 'less than' or 'no better than' me then I can take what she has to offer and not feel envious. This also works in the reverse. Think of what it's like when someone responds to a compliment by saying, 'What? This old thing?' or 'Oh, it needs a coat of paint'. You feel devalued and the other person has assured that you won't envy them. When I was first in private practice and working from home I used to respond to both compliments and snide remarks from clients about my house or my car by saying that I only had nice things because my parents were dead, which completely missed the point even though it was pretty much true.

Confusion and doubt can also function as defences against envy. Think about it. You can stay in a place of not receiving by always being confused about whether you want something or not or doubtful about its value. This can be quite subtle and often appears under the guise of being 'careful' or 'rational'. Countertransference reactions to this sort of confusion/doubt are specific and involve irritation and impatience rather than the fatigue or bewilderment you might feel when confusion is the result of depression. I once had a supervisee who arrived for her first session and took what felt like an eternity to decide where to sit. I had to stop myself shouting 'Oh, for God's sake just sit down, would you!'

Not celebrating another's success can be a defence against envy. I have a client who feels she must be a 'terrible person' because she is so bitter about the fact that her younger sister has all the things in life that she feels she lacks. It is hard for her to admit that she really wants to see her sister fail at something. Anything. This is a client who comes week after week and tells me, almost gleefully, how awful her life is and how wonderful everyone else's is. Occasionally I hear about this client's success or read about it in the newspaper and am interested that she doesn't let me in on this. My supervisor suggests that she may be trying to protect me from being envied for my success in having made a difference. I haven't figured out yet what to do about it, probably because I find it a bit far-fetched. What I do believe is that she has been reluctant to tell me about her successes – fame even – because she was so used to being envied as a child that on some level she fears I will envy her because she travels in posh circles. I decided to share this thought with her and she was visibly relieved. Not only that, but her litany of complaints has all but ceased.

Arrogant people often talk very openly about how they are envied by others. This is proof of their apparent superiority – 'Of course people envy me. I *am* superior.' Defensively this serves to project envy on to others rather than to experience it. I had a colleague once who went through a phase of telling me that I envied her. I honestly couldn't work out what I was supposed to envy, as what I knew about her life seemed pretty unenviable to me. Years later I discovered that I had something I didn't realize I had that *she* envied in *me*.

Generosity, when not truly from the heart, can also be a way of defending against the envy of others. So can 'not succeeding'. Ruth's mother used to tell her that people wouldn't like her if she won so she would deliberately lose races at school. Just for good measure she would also give her toys away and, later, her money. Despite her mother's efforts Ruth was very successful. As therapy progressed Ruth was able to see that she would regularly sabotage her successes by getting pissed and then beating herself up. Once she was able to make this connection she learned not to drink on the back of a personal or public triumph until she had brought out her potential to let celebration give way to a reason to punish herself. She also realized, when she stopped using drink to protect herself from the envy of others, she was likely to get ill following a success. She regularly travelled around the country and abroad to give lectures and often spent several days in bed with non-specific viruses after she got home. The more successful the lecture the worse the virus. Ruth eventually came to see her own envy, becoming aware of how she used her generosity to compete with others whom she envied. She also came to see that her self-sabotage also protected her from having to compete with others, allowing her to treat those who she secretly saw as having what she believed she could not have with contempt.

Defences against envy can work in two ways, either to defend against an anticipated envious attack from another or to defend against acknowledging one's own envy. I would like to give a bit of attention to the positive side of envy in the therapeutic relationship and in life. Competition, emulation, idealization, and generosity may be defences against envy, but they also play positive functions in learning and in loving. Like shame (see Chapter Seven) envy can also be viewed as distancing and as intensely intimate, depending on the context. It is very tempting to put hurtful remarks down to envy. If we do that we often miss the point that the client is trying to tell us something. A colleague calls it 'honesty's cloak'. From a humanistic perspective envy can be seen as a failed attempt to be 'seen' by the therapist. If we remember that the primary mechanism of envy is projection, then we can see that what feels like envy may have started out as a move towards the therapist, as projection is essentially intimate.

Envy in supervision

Humanistic therapies stress the relational aspects of the therapeutic encounter but let's not forget that psychotherapy and the supervision of psychotherapy is a learning process. People who are envious have great difficulty engaging in learning, either because they fear that what is on offer is somehow tainted or poisonous, or, because, to take something from another who is perceived as being more powerful, triggers feelings of inferiority and dependence.

Envy is one polarity of idealization and emulation. Its healthy form is competition. The situation of being a 'learner' may become quite intolerable because feelings of inferiority provoke hostility towards the 'teacher'. Every 'gift' becomes suspect as if it was designed to show off the superiority of the 'giver'. Envious supervisees tend to find fault with everything the supervisor has to offer. They may do this subtly by refusing or rejecting feedback or advice, or they may attack the integrity of the supervisor. They will either do this to the supervisor's face or do it in the system; for example, in the training group or to the supervisee's colleagues and other supervisees through means that run the gamut from subtle put-downs to out-and-out slander. Trainees may try to appear clever to their peers by spotting the supervisor's weaknesses and otherwise undermining their confidence. Envious supervisees (and psychotherapists!) will often choose to surround themselves with colleagues who are not up to their standard. Another way envy becomes manifest in supervision and training groups is by a trainee claiming superiority to the supervisor/trainer and fighting him for control of the group. When this results in a relentless, intractable attack on the supervisor the supervisory relationship must be brought to an end, although it is often hard to accept 'defeat' in the face of a hostile and threatening supervisee.

Finally, let me just highlight one of the pitfalls of helping supervisees to recognize their own envy when it might be getting in the way of their work. A colleague just said to me with more than a little exasperation, 'I've got my supervisee to see that she's envious and now she feels ashamed. Now what do I do?' Read on.

CHAPTER SEVEN

LIVING WITH THE ENEMY – SHAME IN THE SUPERVISORY RELATIONSHIP*[1]

Introduction

When we were talking about how to approach the subject of shame in supervision we were reminded of a story a colleague once told us. Her seven-year-old daughter and a friend asked our colleague if she could take them to the park the following afternoon. 'I can't,' she said, 'I've got supervision.'

Unwittingly, our colleague was soon to become something of a schoolyard legend. Her daughter was used to this kind of pronouncement but her beautifully literal little friend announced to her classmates the next morning that 'Jenny's mum has x-ray vision. You know, like superman.'

---

*A version of this chapter originally appeared in the *British Gestalt Journal* (Kearns & Daintry, 2000). This explains the use of 'we' instead of 'I' and occasional references to boundary, field, and creative adjustment that seemed to resist my efforts to translate the original into a shared language. I haven't translated or explained the use of the terms 'introject' and 'projection'; when they appear they are to be understood in the general sense and not as 'interruptions' or 'moderations' to contact.

Of course Jenny's friend was on the right track. Supervision *is* a process of seeing-through, albeit with different punctuation. A supervisor 'sees' the client through the supervisee. Supervision is also a process of seeing, through the supervisory relationship and what it evokes in the supervisor and supervisee, possible parallels in the client–therapist relationship. Finally, it is also a process of seeing-through, or beyond, a supervisee's 'growing edges',[2] to their unique potential for doing effective therapy. It is, perhaps, the x-ray vision aspect of the supervisory relationship that increases the possibilities for shame to occur, particularly for trainees.

Shame is a feeling, a quality of 'being'. At its worst, it is acutely debilitating. But it also serves a positive, self-regulatory function in the process of assimilating values and of socialization. Shame exists – we cannot get rid of it. It is a boundary phenomenon that is present in the relationship between two people when one of them 'feels seen' in a particular way. We cannot be in relationship without the possibility of experiencing shame.

Shame and its close relative, embarrassment, are easily evoked in any learning situation. The experience of being observed while experimenting with something new is likely to be uncomfortable, particularly for adults. In our experience, the only way 'through' shame is to feel it, live it, and survive it in the presence of another who is also willing to share her human frailty in the moment. Having said that, we are aware that our focus here may seem to lean towards ameliorating the effects of shame as they occur in the relationships that we have described. We have been influenced by the culture of the institute where we trained and its offshoots, which emphasizes working 'live' with fellow trainees as clients in large group, or 'fishbowl' situations. Trainings that place a high value on this kind of 'performance' are, we imagine, more potentially shaming than those that value a different learning style. We also take the view that our sensitivity to shame phenomena is the inevitable result of focusing our attention over the last ten or so years on supervising trainee therapists in a climate that is increasingly litigious and market driven and, therefore, increases 'performance anxiety' on the part of both the supervisor and the trainee.

We want to attend here to some of the influences of the current climate and of some recent strands of thinking on the practice of psychotherapy and supervision in relationship to shame phenomena. Our thesis throughout this article is that shame is inevitable in training situations. We are interested in how to work to amend our practice to make it less shaming, when that is appropriate, and in how to support a supervisory relationship when shame enters the room.

Humanistic psychotherapy's roots in existentialism lead its practitioners to emphasize personal responsibility and choice. We need to remember that, however empowering it is to be free to choose, the very act of making choices *is* anxiety producing. In other words, acknowledging the *dis*-comfort inherent in the human condition is a necessary part of our work as psychotherapists and as supervisors. This discomfort may manifest itself as shame in both parties to an encounter. We encourage our supervisees not to get caught up in a style of practice laced with the inhibition that would result from thinking, moment to moment, about how they might be shaming their clients but, rather, to recognize the conditions that can breed shame and to be alert to the phenomenology or signs of shame. Thus armed, we believe, they will be supported as practitioners to trust in the process of self-regulatory resolution in relationship.

Two types of shame

We are interested in the two differing perspectives on shame that have recently emerged in the gestalt world. There are those (Lee, 1996; Mackewn, 1997; Wheeler, 1995) who suggest that shame is a social field condition, the opposite of support; and those (Fuhr & Gremmler-Fuhr, 1995; Philippson 1996; Resnick, 1997) who do not believe that the felt experience of shame can be explained sufficiently as simply a lack of support in the field.

We agree that shame *is* sometimes best described as an experience of disconnectedness from the field or the 'other' characterized by a sort of turning against the self and withdrawal. At other times it is an intensely personal and painful experience of connectedness to 'other' or to what is projected on to 'other'. We see splitting as the primary defence (see Chapter Two) in the experience of shame. However, we understand the 'felt sense' of shame to be different depending upon the person's developmental 'story'. In the first instance there is no felt connection with 'other'. Rather, the other's perceived displeasure, or even disgust, is taken on and is processed in the body and felt as self-disgust. In the second instance the person who feels shame experiences an over-intense connection with other based on his felt sense of having fallen short of the ideal that he has projected on to them. We believe that the experience of shame that is processed in the body is developmentally earlier than the experience of shame that has its origins in idealization and projection. Throughout this chapter, for expediency's sake, we will apply Bohr's (1934) principle of complementarity and use the term 'shame' to name both kinds of experience.[3]

A review of the literature

Interestingly, shame phenomena have received very little attention in the general literature on supervision. Much attention is paid, both to developmental levels of the supervisor and supervisee (Holloway, 1987; Stoltenberg & Delworth, 1987) and to the process and structure of supervision (Carroll, 1996; Hawkins & Shohet, 1989; Yontef, 1996). Talbot (1995) and Alonso and Rutan (1988) have written about shame in the supervisory relationship from a psychodynamic perspective, the latter focusing primarily on the clinical trainee's vulnerability to humiliation through identification with their client's unconscious processes.

Nathanson (1987) has written that we are not lacking in examples of shame but that open discussions of the issues surrounding shame have eluded us as a profession until recently. Shame has been in hiding, and this is the very breeding ground in which it thrives. Tomkins (1963) published his seminal work on shame some twenty years before others addressed it as a clinical issue in the psychoanalytic literature. Since Kaufman (1980) there has been an increasing interest in and debate on the subject in the analytic literature and, more recently, in gestalt literature. We hypothesize that shame issues have not eluded us. but that the psychotherapeutic profession has introjected beliefs about perfection and self-disclosure that have supported shame issues to remain undiscussed.

We believe that shame in the supervision of trainees is mostly activated by a complicated web of introjects and projections that link the very real power differential in the relationship with often unspoken expectations: the training institute of the supervisor and supervisee; the supervisor and supervisee of each other; and each of themselves. What begins as a private meeting with a client creates exposure and vulnerability for all concerned.

We want to emphasize that the supervisor is as vulnerable to shame as the supervisee. The supervisor often has the institute or other colleagues metaphorically looking over her shoulder. Recently, one of us received a phone call from a colleague who wanted to offer an opinion about one of our supervisees who had done a piece of live work on a workshop he had run. Although our colleague gave, reportedly, hard feedback about the work to the trainee at the time, he phoned her supervisor 'as a matter of courtesy'. His cordial manner failed to disguise a subtext of criticism of the supervisor's work, through his criticism of the supervisee's 'performance'.

One of the introjects that supports shame in the supervisory relationship also supports an assessment system where criteria are not always well defined. As trainees we experienced, and several of our trainees now tell us that they experience, an expectation for them to be, not just competent and ethical therapists but, also, 'evolved human beings'. We are reminded of a post-qualification training day that we attended where the participants – all experienced therapists – were asked by the trainer to think of something we felt very 'alone with' and to imagine telling it to the person next on our right. The drop in 'temperature' in the room was palpable and the trainer asked what was happening. The nearly unanimous response in a go-round was, 'I can't tell them that. They'll think I'm a bad therapist.'

It has been proposed (Guggenbuhl-Craig, 1971; Miller, 1981) that those of us who are drawn to the practice of psychotherapy have been narcissistically injured, and that one way of hiding this damage is to put ourselves in positions where we can help others. Benjamin (1993) proposes that people with avoidant (or shame-based) personality styles are attracted to the practice of psychotherapy because it provides an opportunity for intimacy from a safe distance. We suspect the profession of psychotherapy has created a fertile breeding ground from shame through its collective reluctance to self-disclose. Even therapists who work within a theoretical framework that supports genuine and open communication between client and therapist keep all sorts of things about themselves 'hidden' from their clients

Power issues in supervision

Psychotherapy is practised in private. The clinician takes this 'private' relationship to supervision. This may happen in a one-to-one relationship or in a small group setting, and will involve playing a tape of the session and/or talking about client work. Either way, the process of supervision is exposing something that *is* private. Even clear contracts between supervisor and supervisees do not prevent the supervisory relationship from being one that can evoke the feeling of being spied on while having a very intimate experience. The supervisory relationship does not only expose 'mistakes'; trainees, from time to time, disclose intimate details about themselves and their process to a supervisor who may have real power to block the trainee's progress.

Supervision can often trigger feelings of dependency, powerlessness, and helplessness. In the practice of supervision of trainee psychotherapists the supervisor–supervisee field is charged with an actual power differential once the requirements of the training institute are brought into focus. The supervisor's job is threefold: to support and to protect the therapist–client relationship; to teach the trainee how to be a psychotherapist; and to assess the trainee's competence. Under appropriate circumstances it is the supervisor's duty to stop a trainee from continuing to train. No matter how much a supervisor supports a more collegial approach, and models making mistakes and surviving them (see Chapter One), this relationship *is* a hierarchical one and, thus, is potentially fertile ground in which shame issues can flourish.

Recognising shame phenomena

The phenomenology of shame takes many forms – self-consciousness, blushing, shyness, embarrassment, feeling 'in disgrace', apathy, hopelessness, blankness, cringing, physically shrinking or freezing, turning away, self-criticism. People who are able to report on their experience of shame in the moment often describe feelings of wanting to disappear. They feel defective, bad, unlovable, unworthy, and are acutely in touch with a core felt sense of feeling 'found out' which makes them pull away from the observing other in order not to feel further exposed.

Defences against shame

A shame response can be seen as a creative way of surviving in a relationship or environment that is perceived as threatening. As supervisors we are most likely to meet shame in the guise of some of these attempt to survive – contempt, blame, envy, anger, despair and self-righteousness.

Contempt

The contemptuous person may feel superior and see others as lesser or inferior beings who are lacking in some way. Contemptuous supervisees often appear to be on a fault-finding mission, attempting to relocate their shame in another in order not to experience it themselves. Their contact style tends to be unemotional and judgemental and can, often, induce others to feel stupid. For example, we have noticed that if the supervisor attempts to heighten a supervisee's awareness of the absence of affect before a working alliance is in place, a dismissive and condescending response can be elicited. A supervisee who is not in touch with her feelings is often defending against shame about feeling. In our experience, supervisees may attempt to blame and shame their supervisor in order to avoid experiencing their own feelings of inadequacy. For example, a beginning trainee was having difficulty getting clinical experience. He blamed the training institute for not making it easier for him; he blamed his supervisor for his needing to get a part-time job to earn money (to pay for supervision), which reduced the time he had available

173

to find clients. Further investigation of his blaming helped him to realise that he felt less good than his fellow trainees and, in fact, imagined that many of them had no trouble finding clients. Some reality checking with the other members of his supervision group helped him to support himself better by learning that getting started is difficult for most people.

Envy

Envy as a defence against shame emerges frequently, particularly in supervision groups, where supervisees will inevitably compare themselves to each other. The supervisor is also a target for envy. A trainee who was struggling financially left supervision recently, noticed a new car in the driveway and remarked, 'So this is what you do with all the money we pay you.' Another sat doodling throughout the check-in while her two fellow trainees reported on new clients who had been referred to them by a member of their training group. When the supervisor inquired about the doodling the supervisee replied sarcastically, 'I'm surprised you noticed me when Richard is talking about such an interesting client.'

Envy (see Chapter Six) diverts attention from the felt experience of being deficient and focuses on the perceived strengths or assets of the other, wanting and despising them at the same time. Envious people are unable to experience the strengths perceived in the other in themselves, and therefore feel hostile and destructive. They feel shame at being 'less-than' and may angrily attack the other's 'more-ness'.

Anger

The anger that erupts as a protection against shame is a distancing feeling that energetically pushes the other(s) away in an attempt to preserve a sense of self-cohesiveness. Feeling powerful can help to defend against the feelings of helplessness that can rush into awareness when previously hidden, 'faulty' aspects of the self are exposed.

The defensive expression of anger and rage takes many forms. One supervisee abruptly threatened to end her supervision arrangements because her supervisor failed to return a phone message – left on a Sunday evening – until the following morning. Another attempted to make a formal complaint against her supervisor who would not support her in continuing in training without taking a year out in which to integrate what she had learnt. This supervisee was later able to see that she had over-reacted from a place of deep woundedness. She spent months painfully depressed while she did battle in therapy with her belief that to slow down meant to fail.

Depression

Depression, as a defence against shame, is often character-ized by feelings of hopelessness, as though the person who feels shame is doomed to never live up to his potential. This is a depression without resentment that can descend when someone feels inadequate in the face of another's achievements. The despairing trainee will find it incon-ceivable that she can be any different. The supervisor must guard against the pull to collude with a supervisee's discouragement, holding the possibility of faith in a successful outcome even if, as in the example above of the trainee who reluctantly took a year out, the successful outcome may mean moving to another theoretical orientation more suited to her. In this instance, the supervisee was finally able to see that her choice to train in a humanistic approach had been unwise. She is now successfully pursuing her goal of being a therapist in solution-focused therapy.

The supervisor's defences

It needs to be said that supervisors are as vulnerable to shame as any one else and are also likely to hide it defensively. As supervisors, we are frequently triggered into our own experience of shame and therefore into our habitual coping styles in its presence.

One of us was recently engaged in an impasse with a supervisee who had just failed a piece of written work that was meant to describe his learning in supervision. The supervisee blamed the supervisor whose own private store of beliefs about not being good enough were activated. She noticed she was having self-righteous conversations with herself, vehemently asserting to herself that she was right to feel indignation at the way she was being treated.

Envy, too, can be in the supervisor's kit bag of defences. We have many trainees as supervisees who are successful professionals in their own right but who are learning to be psychotherapists. Some of our students are brighter, others more gifted, than we are. Supervisors who feel shame about certain areas of their professional knowledge or performance may, unwittingly, hold back a supervisee who is confident in an area in which the supervisor feels lacking.

Socio-cultural context

Having looked at some of the power differentials that support shame to emerge in supervision and at how it emerges and affects both trainee and supervisor, we will turn now to the wider social-cultural context as it influences the supervisory relationship.

Shaming experiences from the past that have been embedded in the supervisee's self-organization are likely to be re-evoked and to become obstacles in the supervisory relationship as the supervisee seeks resolution of a past relational trauma.

Sadly, at least in Britain, education is often traumatic. As supervision has a strong educative component, memories of teachers and teaching methods and associated feelings and experiences will easily be re-stimulated. Although the Eleven Plus was abolished years ago, the culture that supported this examination still has an effect, particularly on those who are over forty when they enter psychotherapy training. One of us was educated in Britain, the other in the USA. In working with trainee therapists both in the USA and the UK, we have observed that one notable difference is that of a candidate's attitude towards being examined. Partly this can be explained by the requirements in most American states for a person who enters psychotherapy training to already have at least a Masters degree, whereas in Britain many trainees in psychotherapy have not been formally examined and assessed since leaving school. As a result, the anxiety and tension that are generated in the period leading up to formal assessment and evaluation can make otherwise competent adults feel like children. Another, more subtle difference is interesting to us. Our experience, both as students and trainers in the USA and the UK, is that students in the former tend to approach examinations as an opportunity to show what they know; students in the UK (and this includes adult trainees) tend to see an examination as a system designed to 'catch then out' by exposing what they *don't* know.

Fuhr and Gremmler-Fuhr (1995) have written about how shame is stimulated by the concentrated attention of others. They see shame as a natural companion to the process of learning, particularly because people tend to feel uncomfortable when being scrutinized by others while experimenting with something new. These conditions for discomfort are the norm in humanistic trainings that focus on 'working' in front of the training group. Avoiding shame under these circumstances, which emphasize exposure and 'performing', is impossible. Likewise, these conditions apply to supervision, individually or in groups. The potential for embarrassment or more deeply felt experiences of shame to emerge will depend on several conditions: the expectations of the training institute of both trainee and supervisor, the supervisor's own educational deficits or surfeits, the supervisee's previous experience of learning and the availability of support 'in the room'.

Heidi is a qualified counsellor and a trainee psychotherapist. She has overcome severe dyslexia to have a thriving practice as a counsellor and to design and run training courses. Over the course of a long supervisory relationship with Heidi, her supervisor was made aware of the issues of shame inherent in the possibility of success. Heidi's educational journey was a painful one. Her dyslexia was not identified until she was twenty-five. As a child she learnt to avoid her feelings of inadequacy and failure by acting the joker in class and being a leader amongst those who regularly played truant. By the time Heidi discovered she was dyslexic her ground was already filled with what she had *not* accomplished (she achieved no 'O' levels), and her sense of competence was entangled with the creative adjustments she had made to defend against her own and others' belief that she was stupid.

When Heidi began to train as a psychotherapist she began to 'forget' appointments with her supervisor, who had previously supervised her counselling practice. A pattern of absenteeism began to emerge, particularly if getting help with writing one of several mini-case studies required for her training was on the agenda. When her supervisor facilitated her in looking at this pattern Heidi became aware of how the experience of being seen for having *actually* succeeded was shaming. She could hear her mother saying 'Don't blow your own trumpet' each time she got ready to tackle a new experience. Gradually, as her successes became more embedded in her self-organization and she was able to be more aware of how her original survival decisions did not meet her present needs, her ability to let herself be seen has grown alongside her increasing ability to experience what she called 'being really good at something'.

Supervisors who tend to feel shame about their educational deficits can get entangled with someone who feels similarly shamed. Through understanding our own educational wounds as well as those of our supervisees, it is more possible to offer a different and healing experience in supervision.. As supervisors we need to honour, for example, the person's experience of having been shouted at and humiliated at school for getting something wrong and show, through modelling, that this is not going to happen in our relationship.

Family shame

Although shaming is frequently used as a child-rearing technique, it is important to differentiate between 'toxic' shame and existential shame. The latter is an innate affect, a felt sense that we have let ourselves and/or others down. It is how we know that we have hurt someone and is, perhaps, the beginning of our capacity for inclusion. People who do not experience shame – such as those with anti-social personality features – are not able to experience empathy for another.

Supervision can re-stimulate childhood memories of feeling awkward and incompetent compared to adults. If the child's primary caretakers met this awkwardness sensitively, then she will have access to an experience of shame that was transformed into an opportunity for growth. If, however, the child's consistent experience in relationship has created a weakened sense of self, then the experience of shame is more painful – perhaps unbearable – and it is as a result of this toxic overload that shame emerges as a defence. These defences then become both the self-protectors and the gaolers of the original shame memories. Because these original memories rarely emerge into awareness, they get held in a time warp that often bears no relation to the present relational field.

For example, Beth, who was just starting to see clients, brought a tape-recording of a session to her third meeting with a new supervisor and a new group. The supervisor, having gone through this process during her own training, was well aware of how exposing it can feel. Eager to make this a better first experience for her new supervisee than her own had been, she alerted this supervisee to some of the pitfalls of playing tapes in supervision. She told the group stories about forgetting to locate the place on the tape ahead of time and spending precious supervision time trying to find the right place or, worse, forgetting to listen to the tape beforehand and finding that the microphone hadn't worked. The supervisor suggested to Beth that she use the tape player installed in the room and that she think care-fully about what she wanted from the supervision group with regard to feedback. She said that it would be fine for Beth to ask for positive feedback only, as this was her 'debut'. So determined was the supervisor that Beth would have a good experience that she forgot all about her, lost in a reverie of reminiscence and projection! Beth played the tape, received feedback and all 'seemed' to be well.

When she returned a fortnight later Beth made it clear that she had *not* felt taken care of during the previous session. Her recollection that the supervisor had insisted that she use the tape recorder in the room had so confused her that she had gone home feeling shaken and humili-ated. Beth's supervisor, by anticipating what Beth *should* need rather than asking her what she *did* need, had inad-vertently triggered a developmental shame-memory in Beth, leaving her feeling wide open and unprotected. Often shame-provoking incidents occur when one person is too centred in her own perspective and out of touch with the other's experience.

However, the supervisory relationship can also provide ample opportunity for healing old wounds when the relationship has enough historical support for the supervisee to risk experiencing discomfort in order to do battle with old ways of feeling. Heidi, for example, was able to realize an ambition she never thought was possible because she was able to reinvent herself through a supportive and challenging relationship with her supervisor that has helped her to trust in the support that was available to her.

Transference and countertransference

As supervisors, we have to be able to differentiate between emotional responses that are triggered in both parties in the relationship that originate in a historical relationship and those reactions that signal rupture in the present relationship. For example, Beth's supervisor's spontaneous feelings of warmth and compassion towards her for having inadvertently shamed her were genuine feelings for another human being. However, when Beth returned to the next two sessions, still palpably angry and resentful, the supervisor's warm feelings turned into frustration, anger, and coldness. To the supervisor Beth became more and more entrenched, and seemed determined to remain 'wounded'. The supervisor realized that she was beginning to feel with Beth similarly to how she felt with her mother, who often adopted a martyr-like approach to life. Once she was able to differentiate the past from the present she was more supported to identify Beth's neurotic attempts at contact. Having done so she was able to put the structured boundary of supervision back in place, to move away from a process that could have become inappropriately therapeutic, and to begin to relate to Beth as a bruised trainee.

With another supervisee, Felicity, the complicated and stormy supervisory relationship was getting in the way of attending to her clients. The supervisor worked closely and phenomenologically with Felicity, who became aware that she was projecting a close friend on to the supervisor. It emerged that the relationship with this close friend had broken down and she had never been able to resolve the unfinished business, which left her feeling angry and resentful. If transferential phenomena are persistent and pervasively negative, the supervisor may identify with the projections in spite of her good intentions. The process of sorting this out must not become the focus of supervision or it is likely that the supervisee's work with clients will become background and will suffer from neglect.

Additionally, when the boundary of supervision is invaded by therapy without a verbal contract with the supervisee for this to happen, there is a potential for shaming. An inexperienced supervisor found this particularly challenging with a young supervisee who would arrive for supervision in a very distressed state. Through her own supervision the supervisor eventually realized that the supervisee, who had had several years of therapy before training to be a therapist, was now learning how to be a supervisee rather than a client. The supervisor was in the early stages of learning to be a supervisor, and for a while they were both in rather a muddle until the supervisor named the field conditions. This made space for the supervisee to hear that the primary purpose of supervision was the welfare of her clients. These two 'beginners' were then able to agree a contract for supervision that only included some brief therapeutic intervention if contracted for at the time.

Narcissistic shame

Narcissism's close relationship to shame has been well documented by a number of authors, such as Morrison (1989), Wurmser (1981) and Lewis (1987). In our experience, supervisees whose self-process is fragile (see Chapter Two) tend to find supervision a real challenge, as do their supervisors. Supervisees whose low self-esteem has to be defended against because of the shame that 'exposure' might stimulate, often present as grandiose.

Supervisees with a narcissistic self-process who need to be perfect and to be the 'favourite' supervisee can put much strain on a supervisory relationship. Most trainee psychotherapists struggle with making and owning mistakes. The ones with a more narcissistic self-process will tend to globalize their specific mistakes. For example, 'I need to learn to let my client make her own meaning' can be reframed as, 'I am a bad and useless person'. What might be an ordinary mistake for a beginning therapist sends the more narcissistically challenged plunging from grandiosity to its polarity, despair. They appear to collapse into an abyss of worthlessness and self-loathing.

Lauren, a trainee who has worked with the same supervisor for four years, continues to struggle with her demands on herself to be 'the perfect therapist'. In the early days of their relationship, when Lauren would bring a tape, her supervisor discovered that when she agreed with Lauren's assessment of what she had done well Lauren would beam, and together they basked in her success. However, if the supervisor agreed, or was perceived to agree, with Lauren's negative self-assessment, she experienced an instant break in their relationship. Lauren became devastatingly upset. Her breathing became shallow, her skin flushed, and she reported feeling 'wiped out'. Her supervisor found it difficult to be authentic with her because she felt as though she was either being invited to join in Lauren's self-criticism or to rescue her from her discomfort by praising her.

By resisting the pull and staying 'neutral' she was eventually able to support Lauren to stay with the feelings that were triggered when she experienced a fall from grace in her supervisor's eyes for not being perfect enough. Her supervisor checked with her what it was that she had seen or heard from her that had triggered her shame, and helped her to stay with her present experience in relationship for increasingly longer stretches of time. Although the shame of her 'being-ness' is still heavily overlaid by her 'doing-ness', there has been a marked softening of her expectations on herself as the supervisory relationship has developed. She has a much stronger 'observing ego' and is now aware of her need for adulation from others, including her clients. However, by having her need to be recognized satisfied in other areas of her life she has become less likely to look for recognition from her clients and feels increasingly empowered as a person. By differentiating a 'healthy' from an 'unhealthy' narcissism, she began to heal an injury from the past and to grow as a therapist. Her supervisor also experienced profound healing in this relationship as facilitating Lauren to accept her growing edges helped her to acknowledge and accept her own.

Shame traps for supervisors

We work with supervisees who are in training at a variety of institutes. The supervisory contract with a psychotherapy trainee is, of necessity, 'three-cornered' (English, 1975). The supervisor has a contract with the supervisee about the parameters of their relationship and also has a contract with the training institute. The latter usually – or ought to, in our opinion – involves giving some written assessment of the supervisee's progress and often involves attending meetings of other supervisors and trainers to discuss a trainee's overall progress and any problems encountered.

A supervisor of trainees, in effect, works for the institute, which can sometimes be experienced by the supervisor as critical if a supervisee does not perform up to standard. The possibility of being exposed as having failed as a supervisor, or of some 'hidden' aspect of the self of the supervisor emerging through the presentation of a difficult relationship with a supervisee in one of the Supervisors Meetings, makes these gatherings, designed for the benefit of the trainee, potentially shaming for the supervisor. Worse still, trainees who are having a difficult time in supervision – possibly as a result of unresolved transferential issues – will often 'bad mouth' the supervisor to their peers and their trainers. Understandably this can trigger shame in the supervisor, who would prefer to be seen as competent by the organization and her peers. (See Chapter One: 'The transferential web'.)

In our experience, the values of the supervisor and those of the training institute are often at odds. As supervisors our main concern is to produce competent, ethical practitioners. That is, of course, one of the institute's main concerns. However, the reality of the market leads training institutes to make decisions that would appear to be financially driven rather than competence driven. For example, a trainee who is allowed to progress to a higher level of training without gaining enough clinical experience will always be at a disadvantage. Frequently, though, a trainee *is* allowed to progress to the next year against the advice of her supervisor. Chaos can emerge in a supervision group when one of its members has just 'squeaked through' to the next year of training. The other members are often 'silenced' because they are afraid to voice what they observe and experience in relationship to their colleague. We believe that this phenomenon is supported in part by the trainees' fear of questioning the institute's judgement and, in part, by a lack of faith in the system. As one trainee recently said when reporting that a fellow trainee, who seemed obviously incompetent to her, was allowed to continue on to the next year, 'If they let him through, I wonder if I can believe the feedback I get about being good at what I do.' An adherence to clear assessment criteria in spite of market forces would not only make the supervisor's job easier, but would decrease the potential for shame to both parties to the supervisory relationship.

We believe that shame is an inevitable component of all supervisory relationships. Supervisors must have a commitment to understanding their own shame triggers as well as of their capacity to shame others and to recognise when that has happened. Equally important, is to help trainee therapists to support themselves in tolerating anxiety and low levels of shame. The failure to do this will, we fear, result in producing a generation of therapists who have become separated from humanism's existentialist roots: the belief in the inherent pain of freedom, choosing and responsibility and the potential for healing in human relationship.

Notes

1. Perls (1947) refers to shame as one of the 'Quislings of the organism'. (Quisling was a Norwegian who collaborated with the Nazis.) Perls saw shame as the first line of defence, allying itself with the unfriendly environment – the enemy – and not with the healthy expression of the organism.
2. 'Growing Edge' is gestalt-speak for areas for improvement. It is also the name that we gave to our post-qualification training activities.
3. Bohr, a physicist, proposed that light was neither a wave nor a particle but that it could be both simultaneously, depending on the experience of the observer.

CHAPTER EIGHT

TRAUMA, MEMORY, AND THE BRAIN*

In my early teens I, like most other Americans, was bombarded night after night on the six o'clock news by the atrocities taking place in Vietnam. It was hard to imagine then that anything good would come out of America's extended 'police action' there. Once the Americans pulled out of Vietnam and turned their attention to the Middle East, and to the oil that replaced Communism as the new national obsession, Vietnam was rapidly forgotten. In New York, where I lived, returning war veterans were usually honoured by a hero's welcome complete with what's known as a 'ticker-tape' parade through the financial district. This did not happen for the Vietnam veterans until ten or so years after they came home, once someone made the connection that the way the young men who had fought in Vietnam were ignored on their return by a nation that was on some level ashamed to acknowledge them contributed to their post-traumatic experience. Just like the soldiers who returned from the First World War suffering from 'shell shock' spurred an interest in the clinical treatment of trauma, so

---

*This is intended as an absolutely basic introduction to complex issues. Research into trauma and its effects and treatment is available and regularly updated at www.trauma-pages.com. You will also find many of the articles mentioned here.

did the Vietnam vets. Three out of four who had experienced heavy combat with its associated atrocities suffered symptoms of what came to be known as post-traumatic stress disorder (PTSD).

The diagnostic category of PTSD first appeared in the *DSM III* in 1980, thanks to van der Kolk and others who worked with Vietnam veterans and to persistent lobbying of the American Psychiatric Association by the veterans themselves.

Once the diagnosis existed it was also applied to women who had been raped and/or sexually abused and who, thanks to the women's movement, were given a voice to speak out about their experiences.

Van der Kolk & McFarlane (1996, p. 9) describe six 'critical issues' that are common in people who have PTSD:

(1) they experience persistent intrusions of memories related to the trauma, which interfere with attending to other incoming information;
(2) they sometimes compulsively expose themselves to situations reminiscent of the trauma;
(3) they actively attempt to avoid specific triggers of trauma-related emotions, and experience a generalized numbing of responsiveness;
(4) they lose the ability to modulate their physiological responses to stress in general, which leads to a decreased capacity to utilize bodily signals as guides for action;
(5) they suffer from generalized problems with attention, distractibility, and stimulus discrimination; and
(6) they have alterations in their psychological defence mechanisms and in personal identity. This changes what new information is selected as relevant.

The main symptoms of PTSD are hyperarousal, constriction, and intrusion. 'Hyperarousal' means elevated levels of general anxiety and of the anticipation of danger. People with this symptom usually have what's called a heightened startle response to formerly benign stimuli in the environment as well as a panicky response to things that remind them of the trauma. 'Constriction' is what happens to the rabbit in the headlights. He appears to be preparing to meet his maker but he is more likely to be in a detached state of consciousness similar to an hypnotic trance. This is also called dissociation. Traumatized people who cannot spontaneously dissociate – which is one of the body's natural ways of surviving the intolerable – often attempt to produce similar results by using drugs or alcohol. 'Intrusion' is the term given not just to intrusive memories and dreams but also to the way traumatized people relive the trauma, not just in their minds but in their actions. Post-traumatic child's play is obsessively repetitive, which is why play therapies are used to discover if or how a child has been abused by a carer. Traumatized adults can find themselves re-enacting the trauma in a disguised form without any awareness that that's what they're doing (see 'Anil', p. 212).

Sarah

Sarah was a wife, mother, and the manager of a small, rural branch office of a bank. Around eleven o'clock one morning, after she had just done a run-through of safety procedures with her staff of two, a man with his head completely covered in black cloth and holding a gun appeared at the counter demanding money. One of the clerks completely froze where she was standing and stayed like that until the robber left the premises. The second clerk did exactly what she was asked to do and did not appear to be in the least bit afraid of the gunman. Later it was revealed that she had wet herself while appearing calmly to take the money out of the till and remembering to trip the silent alarm. Sarah says that her main concern was for the safety of the two young women in her charge. She managed the situation extremely well and spent the rest of the day dealing with the many inquiries from police and head office.

Of the three women present during the robbery only Sarah carried on working at the branch. The one who froze just went home and never came back. The one who wet herself while outwardly appearing the picture of calm became pregnant, having theretofore loudly proclaimed her plan never to have children. Sarah developed PTSD that would have prevented less well-resourced people from carrying out simple daily tasks, never mind running a branch office. Not wanting to seem as though she couldn't cope, and secretly fearing she was going mad, she managed to hide her symptoms from everyone but her husband.

Sarah found herself unable to concentrate and was very easily startled by noises that she normally didn't notice at all, like the slamming of a car door. She began to have fears that the robber knew where she lived and begged her husband to let her stay in a hotel where she'd be safe. She knows now that this was irrational but, at the time, it seemed to her the only possible solution. For months after the robbery she would have panicky symptoms whenever she saw a man in a balaclava – which she did from time to time on the telly – or heard the sound of a motorcycle.

It was seven months after the raid before she consulted her GP. It was another year before she was able to arrange some counselling. The counsellor visited her at home, did an assessment, and heard that Sarah was most troubled by a fear that a man in a black hood would appear at the window. The counsellor suggested that Sarah's husband should wear a black hood while they were at home in the evenings! Sarah's husband sent that counsellor packing and Sarah had to wait another five months before being referred to a Consultant Psychotherapist in the Cognitive Behavioural Psychotherapy Department of a local hospital.

Sarah improved in therapy but was eventually retired on medical grounds because she was unable to go anywhere near her workplace without experiencing panic attacks. Since retiring to rural France, where she feels safe, Sarah has had no further symptoms of PTSD. When asked what she found most helpful in recovering from her post-traumatic symptoms she said that being taken seriously by the therapist, combined with being given information about what was going on in her brain, helped her to believe she could get through it. She also had the support of a strong and loving husband who had the good sense to tell the counsellor who suggested that he wear a balaclava around the house where to put it.

The neuro-biology of trauma

Sarah's experience is that she got the most relief from her anxiety about her symptoms of PTSD when someone finally gave her some information about what was going on in her brain and body. You may find it helpful to have

193

this information to hand when working with clients with PTSD in order to share it with them:

Clinical studies have shown that some people who are exposed to extreme stress develop long-term changes in their hormonal and brain systems. The effects on the amygdala and cortical structures of the over- sensitisation of the noradrenergic system seems to explain in part the symptoms of hyperarousal and re-experiencing of physical symptoms of trauma. Exposure to traumatic events increases the secretion of the stress hormones adrenaline and noradrenaline leading to a heightened startle response and to a corresponding increase in heart rate and blood pressure. This helps to explain the spontaneous anxiety and fear reactions of people with PTSD.

People with PTSD also have abnormally low levels of the stress hormone, cortisol, and abnormally high levels of the neurotransmitters epinephrine and norepinephrine. In conditions of every day stress cortisol limits the activation of norepinephrine, the chief function of which is to activate the hippocampus, the part of the brain that organizes and stores long-term memory. The effects of over-production of norepinephrine may explain why people generally can remember emotionally arousing events better than other less charged events. Under extreme stress, norepinephrine may lead to the storing in the hippocampus of abnormally intense and vivid memories that are then experienced as flashbacks or intrusions.

Endogenous opiates, the body's natural pain suppressors, appear to ease the effects of trauma through emotional numbing and 'amnesia' which may explain why people who suffer the long-term effects of trauma become 'addicted' to substances and activities such as cutting that arouse the secretion of opiates in the brain. What the psychotherapist may see as self-harm may be an attempt at self-cure by the client.

Studies have also shown an increase in levels of thyroid hormones that seem to correlate to the severity of hyper-arousal symptoms. Technology through Magnetic Reson-ance Imaging (MRI) allows researchers to actually see into the brain and shows a reduction in the size of the hippocampus in both war veterans and in women who have been subject to childhood sexual abuse. This may explain two phenomena: enhanced reactivity to events in the here and now as though they were the traumatic event itself, as well as gaps in or absence of autobiographical memory.

Memory

Memory is a process of reconstruction and, as such, involves some degree of distortion and the perspective of the rememberer. This reconstruction is also field-dependent, by which I mean that it is dependent on factors in the environment and within the mind of the rememberer, and is therefore inaccurate as it is the past set in a new context. People can sincerely believe that they have remembered something but have actually been told it or seen it in a photograph. Try it.

Find a picture of yourself as a child and elaborate on the background details to the story it freezes in time. What did you have for breakfast that morning? How did you choose what you were going to wear? Now replay the story you have just told yourself in your mind and see if it feels any different from a 'real' memory. What I'm trying to do is to build a picture of how fragile the process of remembering is and how equally fragile is the process between a client and therapist when the therapist 'digs' for memories. This is not only because by digging the therapist can unwittingly add her spin on the story, but also because some things are available to be remembered because they have been split off for the client's protection when young. And even working to heighten a memory that the client has 'recovered' and brought to therapy will more than likely increase the client's level of psychic distress and may lead to enacting rather than assimilation.

Siegel (1999) defines memory as 'the way past events affect future function' (p.24). The brain is composed of a web of neurons that allow learning to occur. The pattern of how the neurons have been fired in the past affects how they fire in the future. Hebb's (1949) 'axiom' tells us more about this process: circuits that fire together wire together. Each brain is unique and has a unique structure and function that is shaped by each person's experience. No two people remember the same event in exactly the same way. How we recall the past is determined by which components of the brain are activated in the future. As Siegel reminds us , there is no 'storage closet' in the brain where old memories are taken out. Each memory is a new activity in the present moment.

Think of a place you have visited. You may be able to recall how it looked, how it felt, what it was called, where it was and why you were there. You may also be able to recall what you did and how *you* felt both emotionally and physically. Sometimes you can only remember that you were there and nothing about what you did and how you felt. The remembering of why you were there may be due to somebody reminding you and not to a spontaneous association. Remembering is not the reactivation of an old

196

memory or 'engram' – the original impact of an experience on the brain – but, as Siegel says

> the construction of a new neural profile with features of the old engram and elements of memory from others with features of the old engram and elements of memory from other experiences, as well as influences from the present [environment and] state of mind. [Siegel, 1999, p. 28]

Complicated isn't it?

As seen in the example above, there are many ways of remembering but basically there are two types of memory, implicit and explicit. Memories that are implicit do not require conscious processing and are located in the *amygdala* and other *limbic* regions. The brain creates mental models or 'schema' so that we can remember one thing by more than one sense. Stern describes how the baby first knows mother's nipple by its mouth but over time learns to recognize it as a nipple by its hand and by its eye and long before it has any idea what it is or is called. It just *knows* what it is. Implicit memory anticipates rather that plans the future and is the type of memory associated with projection and transference. It also makes it possible for us not to have to learn the same thing over and over again.

Explicit memories are context dependent and are located in the hippocampus, which is the part of the brain that encodes and retrieves information, giving us a sense of time and space. These memories also get filtered through the implicit memory system. Someone has just interrupted me to ask the name of a colleague of whom I was thinking only a few hours before. I cannot remember her name because my attention is elsewhere, but I do have some implicit memories of the woman. She scares me a little. The current field conditions (I'm trying to write

197

a chapter for my book) combined with powerful implicit memories (when I try to think about her I feel anxious) combine to make her disappear from my explicit memory system. I'm confident she'll be back so I'll stop trying to remember and wait for her to appear.

Things that we think about as fact are stored in explicit memory and do not occupy the front of our minds, or 'working memory', otherwise we'd be bombarded with useless information. Experiences that involve little emotional intensity have a greater chance of being 'forgotten'. If an experience is emotionally overwhelming the processing of explicit memory may be impaired, which may account for traumatic memory appearing as intrusive, in flashbacks or dreams.

Allan Schore

Of all those who are doing research in and writing about affective neuroscience, Allan Schore's work seems to me to be the most relevant to the practice of psychotherapy and I'm going to attempt to summarize the main points of his paper on early relational trauma and brain development, the full text of which can be found at http://www.trauma-pages.com/schore-2001b.htm

In a ten-year study of the developing brain, Schore has made discoveries that prove what some schools of psychotherapy have hypothesized all along: that we are motivated by impulses that are unconscious or out of awareness, that these impulses are relational and that injuries in the process of attachment between infant and mother can only be healed face to face, right brain to right brain. The human brain grows and changes in relationship with another brain. That first brain belongs to the primary caretaker and it is a psychotherapist's brain actively in relationship with the client's brain – not theory or technique – that heals early relational damage.

The essential task of the first year of life is the creation of a secure attachment bond between the infant and the primary caregiver. By eighteen months it looks to the untrained eye pretty much how it will always look. The first growth spurt is in the right brain, the part of the brain that governs affect. The left brain goes into a growth spurt from about eighteen months, but the right brain is dominant for the first three years or life. At four years the left brain becomes dominant and remains so for life.

Mother's face is the most potent visual and emotional stimulus in the child's world. What Schore calls 'affect synchrony' acts as an interpersonal matrix by organizing the circuits in the prefrontal areas of the infant's right brain that are involved in affect regulation.

Due to its position at the interface of the cortex and subcortex, the orbitofrontal cortex sits at the apex of the limbic system, which also includes the lower limbic areas of the amygdala.

The orbitofrontal cortex is the 'Chief Executive' of the social-emotional brain and controls behaviour, especially in relation to emotion. The brain's right hemisphere is dominant for unconscious processes because it stores an internal working model of the attachment relationship that determines a person's characteristic approach to affect regulation. (See 'Attachment theory', pp. 202–204). It acts as a 'recovery mechanism' that monitors and regulates duration, frequency, and intensity of both positive and negative affect states. It is also instrumental to the empathic perception of emotional states in others.

The 'good enough mother' that Winnicott described permits her baby access after a separation and responds appropriately and promptly to the infant's emotional expressions. She also allows for the interactive generation of high levels of positive affect in shared playing.

An abusive caregiver not only plays less with her infant but also induces traumatic states of enduring negative affect. She is inaccessible or unreliable in times of stress. Instead of soothing her baby she induces extreme levels of stimulation and arousal and, because she provides little or no interactive repair, the infant's intense negative states last for long periods of time. If the infant has to endure highly charged negative emotional states biochemical changes will take place in its developing brain. It is easy to imagine what happened to my client Ruth's (see below and Chapter Four) brain when as a toddler she was left to scream and scream, night after night. The developing brain deals with these unbearable anxieties through the mechanisms of hyperarousal and dissociation, or what Schore calls 'the escape when there is no escape'. High levels of the stress hormone cortisol are produced and alter the growth of the development of the limbic system leaving permanent, physiological reactivity. It is possible to see Ruth's drinking as an attempt to manage unbearable anxiety, the origin of which she had no conscious memory.

Disorganized toddlers show higher cortisol levels than all other attachment categories (Main and Solomon, 1986). Because a child inevitably seeks a parent when distressed or frightened, any parental behaviour that directly distresses or alarms the child places him in an 'irresolvable paradox' in which he can neither approach the parent, shift his attention elsewhere or escape. These infants are hyperaroused because the sympathetic nervous system that activates heart rate, respiration, sweating, alertness is dominant in first year of life. The parasympathetic nervous system, involved in impulse control and self-soothing, only comes into its own in second year. Schore sees shame as the relationship between these two systems and describes affect regulation as the 'accelerator and the brakes.' When the brakes go on too soon or not soon enough the psyche suffers.

The good news is that the limbic system is the most '*plastic*' area in the cortex, which means it can be remoulded in later life. Psychotherapy interventions must directly access the right brain (Siegel, 1999, p. 299). The therapist, on both an unconscious and conscious level, must act as an interactive monitor and regulator of the client's dysregulated states. The key to this is the therapist's ability to tolerate uncertainty, allow protest, not just hear but feel despair, and hold the client at moments of explosive rage as well as at moments of implosive collapse and withdrawal. This involves the therapist being able to tolerate intense and enduring negative affect states such as shame, hopelessness, and helplessness.

The therapist also needs to provide a context in which both she and her client can experience and interactively regulate the positive states of interest and joy. This is more complex than just support or empathic mirroring, because there may be no receptors to receive positive communications – even though the client may need the love she never had she is not in a position to receive it.

It is important to remember when working with clients who were 'traumatized' as infants that high levels of positive affect are threatening. Offering accurate empathy and pushing for 'feelings' with these clients will drive them deeper into withdrawal and helplessness. The work can feel painstakingly slow. The therapist needs to remember that the client is taking in as much information as he can bear from the therapist's facial reactions and tone of voice. In the early stages of therapy the words don't matter nearly as much as the non-verbal language that accompanies them.

Attachment theory

Research done by Schore and others has confirmed many theories about how people tick, particularly attachment theory. It is generally accepted that people with histories of secure attachment (Bowlby, 1969) respond to and recover from trauma better than the rest of us. This is because trauma commonly brings about a partial and temporary collapse of the ability to regulate emotion and of the *mentalizing capacity* (Fonagy & Target, 1997). This basically refers to our ability to reflect on our own and other's experience. If someone is about to run you over in the street you don't spend a second imagining what it must be like to be so stressed and aggressive. You jump out of the way. And with any luck you pick yourself up and walk on, shaken. Only later might you discover that you've scraped your knee. And you'll tell someone how some idiot nearly killed you, feeling self-righteous maybe, but not in the least bit self-reflective or empathic. So far so good. The next time you cross the road you will, no doubt, be a bit more vigilant and you'll eventually come to believe that, even though the bus driver may in fact be an idiot, he probably wasn't out to get you that day.

People with complicated or impaired attachment histories can't do this. After the same type of encounter with the same idiot bus driver they may become fixated on what they did to provoke or to deserve the incident and will punish themselves over and over again in their minds for not having been watching where they were going. Or they might come to see all buses as potential predators and anxiously avoid them. Some might even believe that the bus driver *was* trying to kill them. I had a client who tried to get London Transport to write to him to apologize on behalf of one of their drivers, even though my client could not describe the driver in any way that he could be identified and wasn't sure whether it was a number 45 or 236. These are all failures of the mentalizing function. We are not born with the capacity for emotional regulation and we don't get good at it without a primary caregiver who can read and respond to our emotional signals, moment to moment. Our past experiences with our primary caregiver – usually mother – form 'internal working models' (Bowlby, 1973) which form the basis of how we relate to ourselves and others in times of stress. No mother or primary caregiver can be perfectly attuned to her baby. To help with the reality of having to soothe themselves infants need to develop the capacity to conjure up a good enough, soothing mother, or the feelings associated with mother when she is not around or when she gets it wrong

You may be familiar with Ainsworth's (Ainsworth, Blehar, Waters, & Wall, 1978) 'Strange Situation' experiments, in which infants who were playing in a room occupied also by their mother and a stranger were left alone with the stranger for a brief while and then mother returned. Infants who had 'secure' attachments to mother played and explored the room contentedly in her presence, became anxious when left alone with the stranger and sought comfort from and were soon reassured by mother when she returned. Those infants who appeared to be less anxious when left with the stranger and who also did not appear to seek comfort from mother when she returned were termed 'anxious–avoidant'. Others, termed 'anxious–resistant' were limited in their ability to play and explore when mother was present. They were highly distressed by her absence but were not comforted by her return and appeared to reject mother's attempts to soothe them. The anxious–avoidant children shut down on their emotions under stress while the anxious–resistant children loudly expressed their distress, seeming desperate for contact on the one hand and actively dismissing it on the other.

A fourth group of infants fell into the 'disorganized–disoriented' category. These were the children who froze or engaged in repetitive movement such as hand-clapping or, more distressingly, head-banging when mother left the room, which they continued well after she returned. Mother was someone who was feared as well as a source of comfort. These children were thought to have had a history of severe neglect or physical or sexual abuse.

Complex PTSD

Janet, a contemporary of Freud, noticed that people who had been traumatized became arrested in some way. Freud observed similar phenomena in his patients and, initially, came to the conclusion that their 'hysterical' symptoms were caused by having been seduced in childhood, causing them to be 'doomed to repeat' the original trauma rather than to remember it. He called this the 'repetition compulsion' and based much of his technique on the belief that if his patients could remember the original trauma they would be cured of their symptoms.

Humanistic therapies have their version of Freud's theory. Perls based his gestalt therapy on the concept from gestalt psychology of 'unfinished business', meaning that the ego seeks closure and will repeat past experience in order to complete it or 'close the gestalt'. TA's 'racket system' is a model of how people often live in the present as though it were the past. Both of these therapies share with Freud the view that remembering the past will produce change in the present. This has not been my experience in therapy and it has not been borne out in my clinical practice either. I can think of many clients who had vivid memories of childhood abuse who still lived in the present as though it were the past. Van der Kolk (1989) says that clinical experience shows that clients rarely gain mastery over the past by repeating it until it is remembered.

Herman (1992) has suggested the term Complex PTSD to describe those clients who were exposed to repeated trauma as opposed to a traumatic event. Although the term primarily refers to people who endured captivity, such as prisoners of war, or situations where they were under another's total control, such as prostitution, domestic violence, or child physical or sexual abuse, I believe it can be a useful lens through which to view those clients who, though otherwise high-functioning, resort to compulsive behaviours under stress. As I said in Chapter Two, the diagnosis of borderline personality disorder is often given to people – particularly women – who were seriously abused as children. Herman (1992), Kroll (1993) and others have written about the treatment implications of working with PTSD borderlines and I encourage you to familiarize yourself with their thinking when working with this type of client.

In my work with addictions and eating disorders I have become interested in clients who have access to certain memories, are able to connect the past to the present, and still persist on a path to self-medication or even self-destruction. In Chapter Six we looked at Rosenfeld's conceptualization of 'a gang in the mind' to understand the destructive mechanics of low-self esteem fuelled by envy.

If the results of envy can be described as a sort of intrapsychic guerrilla warfare, the effects of childhood trauma can be conceived as the sentinels of the psyche. Ruth came to describe the part of her that continued to drink compulsively even when she was aware of all of the reasons that she did so as being 'like that poor man they found on an island in the Pacific who didn't know the war was over'. One aspect of the self may be called upon to protect the more vulnerable parts from repeated suffering, even when the actual cause of the suffering is long gone.

Kalsched (2003) describes the effects of childhood trauma and dissociation as like making a pact with the devil, who says to the traumatized child, 'You can go on living but you must leave the baby with me.' I find this a useful way to conceptualize the process of some of my clients, particularly those who turn to food, drink, drugs, or work in times of stress. To paraphrase Kalsched, it's as if one part of the client had to grow up very quickly while another stayed regressed and frozen. As a result, infantile need, fragility, vulnerability, and insatiability co-exist with a narcissistic rage that is often out of the person's awareness.

When Ruth first came into therapy she told me that she needed an exorcism. She felt as though she was possessed by a demon that made her do things that she couldn't accept. She was convinced that this was because something 'terrible' had happened to her that she couldn't remember. Although a well-functioning professional she felt ugly, smelly, like a fraud, and had an inconsistently damaging relationship with alcohol. Her drinking binges at first seemed random. She binged alone but did not always binge, nor did she always have to fight the urge to binge when she was alone. Over time we were able to identify that her drinking was associated not with feeling 'abandoned' but by feeling punished for being needy or for having done something wrong.

Ruth's mother used to proudly tell her that she fed her like clockwork every four hours when she was a baby and that she 'left her to scream it off' when, as a toddler, she cried on being put to bed. Ruth has no implicit or explicit memory of this.

Ruth also remembers being about four or five and being taken to Hamley's by her mother and having a nice day out. She remembers that, when she thought they would be going home, they suddenly took a 'wrong turn' and ended up in the dentist's office. Mum said, 'I have a surprise for you and when it's over you can have a knickerbocker glory.' Ruth was put to sleep with ether and remembers waking and screaming for her mother, who was not there. She also remembers vomiting all night and never getting a knickerbocker glory. Ruth's mother told her that it was nonsense – that she had been there all the time and that she'd taken her for a knickerbocker glory once she recovered from the anaesthetic. Ruth is most emphatic that this was not the case.

When she was thirteen or so and at boarding school she had an emergency operation. Her mother and father were in Italy and her mother did not come back to England. A much-feared relation tended to Ruth. She remembers phoning her mother a few days after the operation and saying, 'It's all right. I didn't cry.' Ruth's mother corroborated this version of events and used to bring up the story at awkward times saying that Ruth would never forgive her for not coming to her, even though her father had been unwell at the time. Ruth said to me, 'It's not as though they didn't have the money to hire him a nurse. She just didn't want to come all the way back to England for me.'

So here we have three different kinds of memories: something Ruth was told but does not remember, an historical event that she and her mother disagreed about, and one that she remembers fairly accurately, putting her own spin on mother's reasons for not coming to be with her. In therapy, through making meaning of each memory, Ruth has come to understand that her drinking was a re-creation of the experiences of screaming and no one being there (she did this alone at night) as well as of soothing herself in the face of the overwhelming guilt she could easily experience when she went into self-imposed 'exile' for not being good enough or for getting something wrong.

Ruth grew and grew in insight on the one hand and in compassion for the infant and child she had been on the other. She was also able to experience powerful feelings of anxiety and depression when her partner would go away on business and she spent evenings and weekends mostly on her own. She stopped turning to drink on these occasions and was able to come to me instead and tell me how dreadful she was feeling. I, for the most part, was able to soothe her, and eventually she became more able to soothe herself. She and I were able to make manifest the part of her that had been split off as a child and came back to life under certain 're-traumatizing' conditions. Ruth came to understand her drinking as re-enactment of childhood trauma; to soothe herself until someone eventually came to help her. She had to keep her parents as 'good' in her mind, even though they were so infrequently there for her.

Fairbairn (1952) was the first to suggest that what was repressed by the child were not intolerable impulses nor intolerably unpleasant memories but intolerably bad objects (parents). He further went on to say that a relationship with a 'bad' parent is felt by the child not only as intolerable, but also as shameful. This may explain why, for example, a child who is sexually abused feels at fault and protects the abuser. Fairbairn believed that the child 'became bad' in order to keep the parent(s) 'good'.

Some general guidelines re how to work

A lack of being able to feel that at least some things in life are predictable and of having some felt sense – even if it is illusory – of being in control are the central issues for people with PTSD. Without this relative sense of safety and predictability it is difficult to make plans and to take action (van der Kolk, van der Hart, & Burbridge, 1995). Put simply, the common factor in people who experience trauma is the inability to process and integrate a single or many distressing experiences.

The goal of psychotherapy with people who have been traumatized is to help the client to acknowledge the reality of what has happened without having to re-experience the trauma. It is not enough to uncover 'lost' memories or just to listen empathically while the client tells the story behind an intrusive memory. Traumatic memory needs to be transformed through being put in a new context or a different story. Van der Kolk and his colleagues remind us that memory in psychotherapy becomes an 'act of creation'; client and therapist together transform what begins as a disturbing record of events into a meaningful narrative that allows the client to accept the past and to live in the present. They propose five stages of treatment, which I've translated into language that I hope sits better with humanistic practice and philosophy.

1. Stabilising and relationship building

No therapy can take place without the necessary conditions. Clients need to be available for psychological contact (Rogers, 1951). With people with simple PTSD this may be relatively straightforward. They may be able to access the traumatic memory and to talk about it with you. With more complicated cases the therapist may need to spend a great deal of time on providing a place of safety and building trust. Clients who are self-medicating with alcohol or non-prescription drugs may need to stop doing that; other clients who are experiencing severe symptoms may need prescription medication in order to manage them enough to be available for therapy. When the client is available to take in information, teaching them about what is going on in their brains and bodies can be an additional support.

This phase of therapy takes as long as it takes. In my experience it often takes years. Techniques for controlling intrusive memories and anxiety can be useful here and may be all the therapist working in short-term treatment has to offer.

2. Naming feeling and body experience

One way of viewing emotions is that they serve the function of 'alerting' us to the existence and potential meaning of 'events'. An event can be a noise, a sensation in the body, human contact or a collection of occurrences in the environment. Krystal (1978) first noted that in people with PTSD emotions seem to lose much of their alerting function. People who have experienced trauma, particularly repeated trauma, lose their capacity to interpret their emotions and experience them more like alarm bells that are experienced as negative, paralysing or re-traumatizing. As a result, feelings become things that must be avoided. This may not be a conscious process, but feelings, particularly those associated with the traumatic event, are split off through a process of dissociation or are somatized or otherwise enacted rather than felt.

People may repeat the trauma in their actions or their dreams before being able to remember its emotional impact. In Chapter Four we looked at the concept of state-dependent learning: what is learnt under one 'state' may be unavailable until the return of a similar state. Both internal states induced by brain chemicals, or alcohol, or drugs and external events that are similar to the original event(s) can trigger someone who experienced traumatic conditions in childhood to feel or to behave as though she is back in the original situation. This may explain why otherwise competent women become like terrified and helpless children in the face of an abusive partner. Van der Kolk (1989) describes war veterans who seem to be unaffected by what they have experienced until they become involved in an intimate relationship and start reliving feelings of loss, grief, vulnerability, and revenge related to the death of a comrade on the battlefield. These feelings may be incorrectly attributed to some element of the current relationship. The therapist needs to help the client to make the connections that his brain has disconnected and eventually to experience the emotions while connecting them to the original trauma. This can often feel like causing a client unnecessary pain, and it is the therapist's job to provide holding for the client as well as to help him to see that there is a purpose to the suffering that he is experiencing in the process of re-connecting to the original pain.

Anil witnessed a terrible accident in which a neighbour's child was decapitated by a delivery van reversing out of the driveway. He watched the whole thing, shouting and waving to the driver trying to get him to stop. He became unable to work and spent his days looking at pornography on the internet. When he became aroused he would run to a local clergyman and beg his forgiveness. Over time Anil was able to tell his therapist that he had had an erection while trying to stop the van from running over the child. He began to see that his obsession with internet pornography was an attempt to seek absolution for having 'pleasure' in the face of such horror as a child's accidental mutilation and death. Once he faced this and the feelings that he had split off he also remembered that he had had similar experiences as a child when he shared a bed with his older sister who used to seduce him.

3. Transformation of traumatic memories and responses

The theory goes that when the client has established and maintained an emotional connection with the therapist, this is translated into an internalized state of safety. Being able to experience or evoke a traumatic memory in new and safe environment in the presence of a trusted other allows the client not to feel overwhelmed by the emotions that have become associated with the trauma. The client can create a new narrative around the traumatic memory that 'transforms' the traumatic incident into an historical event that can be told and remembered without being re-experienced. The therapeutic encounter has, effectively, created – if not a new memory – then a new story *about* the memory.

4. Making new meaning and perceptions of self and other

Once the client has been able to tell a new story to himself and others about the trauma, therapy can address specifically how the trauma has affected his self-worth, his capacity for trust and intimacy, his ability to meet his needs and respond to his impulses. Anil came to understand how the powerlessness he felt in his life grew from his early experience of repeated humiliation by his sister and turned to obsession and self-loathing when he was unable to prevent the death of his neighbour's child.

5. Exposure to new and pleasurable experiences

Part of the recovery from PTSD is being able to have pleasurable and satisfying experiences that are not connected with the trauma. Sarah found pleasure in embracing a new culture; Ruth began to have regular massage and took up swimming as a replacement for drinking when she was alone.

213

Issues for supervisors

As a supervisor I have met clients who have far more complex and challenging presentations than the sort of client I would feel able to take on in private practice. The entry into the UK of people from countries that have been ravaged by war and its associated atrocities means that inexperienced therapists and trainees working in voluntary placements are regularly assigned clients who have been raped, tortured, or otherwise savaged by other human beings.

Trauma is contagious, and supervisors need to be aware of its more pernicious effects. Some of the possible effects on the therapist when working with traumatized clients are similar to the symptoms that the client can experience, such as survivor's guilt, burnout, distraction, fatalism, hypersensitivity, numbing, self-harm, and experiencing symptoms of PTSD.

Wilson and Lindy (1994) have described two types of countertransference that are specific to working with trauma survivors: (1) *avoidant countertransference*, where the therapist becomes detached from the client's story and experience and (2) *over-identification countertransference*, where boundaries that are not tightly maintained lead to the therapist feeling drained, overwhelmed, and ineffective. Just because these types of countertransference reactions are not uncommon in working with clients who do not have a history of trauma, do not dismiss the almost supernatural intensity with which they can be experienced when working with what in other contexts might be described as pure evil.

You might be surprised at how even – and maybe particularly – an experienced practitioner may become over-identified with what Jung calls the 'redeemer archetype' and rationalize all sorts of boundary violations. I was once consulted by a therapist who was so ashamed about how she had overstepped the boundaries when treating a client who had been the victim – and I use that word deliberately – of ritualized abuse that she did not feel able to reveal the extent of her transgressions to a member of her registering organization, of which she was a senior member. Without going into greater detail of the abuse that her client had endured as a child and of the ways the therapist had transgressed her own moral and her organization's ethical code, I will just say that if I hadn't experienced this colleague's distress first-hand I would find the entire story beyond belief. This therapist acted entirely outside the range of what she had come to know without doubt were her human and professional limits. And she had done so because she had not sought any outside support once the details of the abuse were revealed to her because she had come to believe that it would be in the best interest of her client not to do so!

This is an extreme example, but I use it to illustrate an important point: too much empathy and not enough limit-setting is obviously not good for most clients but, more importantly, can lead to the therapist of a traumatized client becoming vicariously traumatized and victimized. As Kalsched (2003) says, 'We have a right to demand that our clients don't drive us crazy too.'

Humanistic trainees often find the concept of setting boundaries difficult to grasp because it feels unkind to usher a weeping client out the door on time or to put a limit on telephone contact outside scheduled appointments. Supervisors need to explain to trainees, who in turn need to explain clearly to their clients, that therapists adhere to boundaries not because we are cold and uncaring but because we are human too and just as capable as anybody else of being overwhelmed.

The therapist who is confronted with things outside their range of experience and, even, imagination, can also go the other way. Danieli (1984) describes the 'conspiracy of silence' that was a not-uncommon early reaction on the part of therapists who were working with survivors of the holocaust, who – for various reasons from disbelief to self-protection – suppressed the clinical material. As a supervisor, I sometimes hear stories that I find difficult to believe, but I have come to be able to tell the difference now between my psyche's efforts to protect me from something I find hard to hear and something that just doesn't ring true. I urge you to practise this so that you will be more able to take appropriate action to protect yourself and to support your supervisees.

By 'appropriate' action I mean steps that range from the professional and practical to the symbolic. Unless you are experienced in working with atrocities and ritual abuse – and I really hope you're not – when one of these instances of inhumanity comes into your consulting room you need to seek some specialist support. Book at least one session – even if by e-mail or on the telephone – with a practitioner from one of the national trauma clinics. Go back into therapy and insist that your supervisee take his difficulties with the work to therapy too. I have also found it helpful to somehow 'ritualize' protection for myself. I keep a bowl of water in my consulting room, which I empty after a session that contains charged material that could get under my skin. Sometimes I burn candles or incense to clear the room. Others smudge the room, or make a loud noise with a percussion instrument or

Tibetan meditation bowl. And I confess that after I saw the therapist who had, in her words, become possessed by her client with the history of ritual abuse, I walked to the rectory of the local Catholic church, got some holy water and sprinkled it around my consulting room and adjoining areas. That worked for me. Be creative about what might work for you.

As a supervisor of humanistic therapists, particularly ones that are inexperienced and fuelled by idealism, I have found it challenging to help my supervisees to consider the possibility that they may need to look at *their* more sadistic or voyeuristic side in order to use these in the service of the client. 'Using' them involves accepting that each of us is capable of cruelty and even killing under the right conditions. Therapists of clients who have been abused may often feel like 'killing' the perpetrator, and need to manage those fantasies so that the client feels safe to air her own. One of my colleagues, who is a gifted writer as well as a psychotherapist, is writing a novel in which she hopes to symbolically bring to justice a man who did horrific things to one of her clients. Another supervisee was able to move beyond a lengthy *impasse* with a client who had been repeatedly sodomized once I wondered if on some level he found it sexually exciting.

REFERENCES (KEY TEXTS ARE MARKED WITH AN ASTERISK)

Ainsworth, M. D. S., Blehar, M. C., Waters, E., & Wall, S. (1978). *Patterns of Attachment: A Psychological Study of the Strange Situation*. Hillsdale, NJ: Erlbaum.

Alonso, A., & Rutan, J. S. (1988). Shame and guilt in psychotherapy supervision. *Psychotherapy*, 25(4): 576–581.

*Ashwin, M. (2000). *Cronos and his Children* (www.human-nature.com/ashwin/)

*Benjamin, L. (1993). *Interpersonal Diagnosis and Treatment of Personality Disorders*. New York: Guilford Press.

*Berke, J. (1988). *The Tyranny of Malice*. New York: Summit Books.

Berne, E. (1964). *Games People Play: The Psychology of Human Relationships*. New York: Balantine Books.

Bloom, C. (1987). Bulimia: a feminist psychoanalytic understanding. In: M. Lawrence (Ed.), *Fed Up and Hungry*. London: Women's Press.

Bohr, N. (1934). *Atomic Theory and the Description of Nature*. Cambridge: Cambridge University Press.

*Bowlby, J. (1969). *Attachment and Loss Vol. 1: Attachment*. London: Hogarth Press and the Institute of Psycho-Analysis.

Bowlby, J. (1973). *Attachment and Loss, Vol. 2: Separation: Anxiety and Anger*. London: Hogarth Press and Institute of Psycho-Analysis.

Bruch, H. (1974). *Eating Disorders: Obesity, Anorexia Nervosa and the Person Within*. New York: Basic Books.

Carroll, M. (1996). *Counselling Supervision Theory, Skills and Practice*. London: Cassell.

Crisp, A. H. (1989). The psychopathology of anorexia nervosa: getting the 'heat' out of the system. In: A. J. Stunkard & E. Stellar (Eds.), *Eating and its Disorders*. New York: Raven.

References

Danieli, Y. (1984). Psychotherapists' participation in the conspiracy of silence about the holocaust. *Psychoanalytic Psychology*, *1*: 23–42.

Deutsch, H (1942). Some forms of emotional disturbance and their relationship to schizophrenia. *Psychoanalytic Quarterly*, *11*: 301–321.

Duker, M., & Slade, R. (1988). *Anorexia Nervosa and Bulimia: How to Help*. Milton Keynes: Open University Press.

English, F. (1975). The three-cornered contract. *Transactional Analysis Journal*, *5*: 383–384.

Erikson, E. (1963). *Childhood and Society*. New York: Norton.

Fairbairn, W. R. D. (1941). A revised psychopathology of the psychoses and psychoneuroses. *International Journal of Psychoanalysis*, *22*:

Fairbairn, W. R. D. (1952). *Psychoanalytic Studies of the Personality*. London: Routledge & Kegan Paul.

*Fairbairn, W. R. D. (1986). The repression and the return of bad objects. In: P. Buckley (Ed.), *Essential Papers on Object Relations*. New York: New York University Press.

Farrell, E. (2000). *Lost for Words: The Psychoanalysis of Anorexia and Bulimia*. New York: Other Press.

Fonagy, P., & Target, M. (1997). Attachment and reflective function: their role in self-organization. *Development and Psychopathology*, *9*: 679–700.

Foster, George M. (1972). The anatomy of envy: a study in symbolic behavior. *Current Anthropology*, *13*(2): 165-202.

Freud, S. (1917). Mourning and melancholia. *S. E.*, *14*: 237–258). London: Hogarth.

Freud, S. (1931). Female sexuality. *S. E.*, *21*: 225–43. London: Hogarth.

Fuhr, R., & Gremmler-Fuhr, M. (1995). Shame in education. *British Gestalt Journal*, *4*(2): 91–100.

Greenberg, A., & Mitchell, S. (1983). *Object Relations in Psychoanalytic Theory*. Cambridge, MA: Harvard University Press.

*Greenberg, E. (1989). Healing the borderline. *The Gestalt Journal*, Fall.

Greenberg, E. (1996). When insight hurts. *British Gestalt Journal*, *5*(2): 113–121.

Guggenbuhl-Craig, A. (1971). *Power in the Helping Professions.* Dallas, TX: Spring Publications.

*Guntrip, H. (1968). *Schizoid Phenomena, Object Relations and the Self.* Karnac.

Hawkins, P., & Shohet, R. (1989). *Supervision in the Helping Professions.* Milton Keynes: Open University Press.

Heather, N., & Robertson, I. (1997). *Problem Drinking* (3rd edn). New York: Oxford University Press.

Hebb, D. (1949). *The Organization of Experience: A Neuropsychological Theory.* New York: Wiley.

*Herman, J. (1992). *Trauma and Recovery.* New York: Basic Books.

Holloway, E. (1987). Developmental models of supervision: is it development? *Professional Psychology, 18*(3): 189–208.

Hunt, W., & Matarazzo, J. (1973). Habit mechanisms in smoking. In: W. A. Hunt (Ed.),. *Learning Mechanisms in Smoking.* Chicago: Aldine (1970).

Johnson, S. (1987). *Humanising the Narcissistic Style.* New York: W. W. Norton.

Johnson, S. (1985). *Characterological Transformation: The Hard Work Miracle.* New York: Norton.

Jellinek, E. M. (1960). *The Disease Concept of Alcoholism.* New Brunswick, NJ: Hillhouse Press.

*Kalsched, D. (2003). Daimonic elements in early trauma. *Journal of Analytical Psychology, 48*: 145–169.

Karpman, S. (1968). Fairy tales and script drama analysis. *Transactional Analysis Bulletin, 7*(26): 39–43.

Kaufman, G. (1980). *Shame: The Power of Caring.*: Rochester, VT: Schenkman.

Kearns, A., & Daintry, P. (2000). Shame in the supervisory relationship: living with the enemy. *British Gestalt Journal, 9*(1): 28–38.

Kernberg, O. (1975). *Borderline Conditions and Pathological Narcissism.* New York: Jason Aronson.

Klein, M. (1937). Love, guilt and reparation. In *Love, Guilt and Reparation and Other Works, 1921–1945* (pp. 306–343). Reprinted London, Hogarth, 1981.

*Klein, M. (1957). Envy and gratitude in infancy. In: *Envy and Gratitude and Other Works.* Reprinted London, Virago, 1988.

221

*Kohut, H. (1977). *The Restoration of the Self.* New York: International Universities Press.

Kohut, H. (1987). Addictive need for an admiring other in regulation of self-esteem. In: M. Elson, (Ed.), *The Kohut Seminars on Self Psychology and Psychotherapy with Adolescents and Young Adults* (pp. 113–132). New York: W. W. Norton.

*Kroll, J. (1993). *PTSD/Borderlines in Therapy: Finding the Balance.* New York: Norton.

Krystal, H. (1978). Trauma and affects. *Psychoanalytic Study of Children,* 33: 81–116.

Kubler-Ross, E. (1969). *On Death And Dying.* London: Collier-MacMillan.

Lacey, H. (1986). An integrated behavioural and psycho-dynamic approach to the treatment of bulimia. *British Review of Bulimia and Anorexia,* 1(1): 19–26.

Laing, R. D. (1990). *The Divided Self: An Existential Study in Sanity and Madness.* London: Penguin.

Lasègue, C. (1873). De l'anorexie hystérique. In: R. Kaufman & M. Heiman (Eds.), *Evolution of Psychosomatic Concepts. Anorexia Nervosa: A Paradigm.* Reprinted New York, International Universities Press, 1964.

Lee, R. G. (1996). Shame and the Gestalt model. In: R. G. Lee & G. Wheeler (Eds.), *The Voice of Shame.* San Francisco: Jossey-Bass.

Lewin, K. (1952). *Field Theory in Social Science.* London: Tavistock.

Lewis, H. B. (1987). Shame and the narcissistic personality. In: D. L. Nathanson (Ed.), *The Many Faces of Shame.* New York: Guilford Press.

Mackewn, J. (1997). *Developing Gestalt Counselling.* London: Sage.

Main, M., & Solomon, J. (1986). Discovery of an insecure–disorganized/disoriented attachment pattern. In: T. B. Brazelton & M. W. Yogman (Eds.), *Affective Development in Infancy* (pp. 95–124). Norwood, NJ: Ablex.

*Manfield, P. (1992). *Split Self/Split Object.* Trenton, NJ: Guilford Press.

Maslow, A. (1970). *Motivation and Personality*, 2nd edn. New York: Harper & Row.

*Masterson, J. (1976). *Psychotherapy of the Borderline Adult: A Developmental Approach*. New York: Brunner Mazel

*Masterson, J. and Klein, R. (Eds.) (1995). *Disorders of the Self*. New York: Brunner Mazel.

*McDougall, J. (1989). *Theatres of the Body: A Psychoanalytical Approach to Psychosomatic Illness*. London: Free Association Books.

Miller, A. (1981). *The Drama of Being a Child*. London: Virago.

Minuchin, S., Rosman, B., & Baker, L. (1978). *Psychosomatic Families: Anorexia Nervosa in Context*. Cambridge: Harvard University Press.

Morrison, A.. P. (1989). *Shame: The Underside of Narcissism*. Hillsdale, NJ: The Analytic Press.

Nathanson, D. L. (1987). A timetable for shame. In: D. L. Nathanson (Ed.), *The Many Faces of Shame* (pp. 1–63). New York: Guilford.

Nhat Hanh, T. (1987). *The Miracle of Mindfulness*. Boston: Beacon Press.

Orbach, S. (1982) *Fat is a Feminist Issue*. New York: Paddington Books.

Orford, J., & Keddie, A. (1986). Abstinence or controlled drinking: a test of the dependence and persuasion hypotheses. *British Journal of Addiction*, *81*: 495–504.

Palazzoli, M. S. (1986). *Self-Starvation*, Northvale, NJ. Aronson.

Perls, F. S. (1947). *Ego, Hunger and Aggression*. Reprinted New York, Vintage Books, 1969.

Perls, F., Hefferline, R., & Goodman, P. (1951). *Gestalt Therapy: Excitement and Growth in the Human Personality*. Reprinted London, Souvenir Press, 1984.

Philippson, P. (1996). A note in response to Richard Erskine on shame. *British Gestalt Journal*, *I. 5*(2): 128–129.

Prochaska. J. O., & DiClemente, C. C. (1986). Towards a comprehensive model of change. In: Miller & Heather (Eds.), *Treating Addictive Behaviours*. Plenum Press.

Prochaska, J. O., DiClemente, C. C., & Norcross, J. C. (1992). In search of how people change: applications to addictive behavior. *American Psychologist*, *47*: 1102–1114.

Prochaska, J. O., Velicer, W. F., DiClemente, C. C., Guadagnoli, E., & Rossi, J. (1991). Patterns of change: a dynamic typology applied to smoking cessation. *Multivariate Behavioral Research, 26*: 83–107.

*Racker, H. (1968). *Transference and Countertransference*. London: Karnac Maresfield Library.

Resnick, R. (1997). The recursive loop of shame: an alternate Gestalt therapy viewpoint. *Gestalt Review, 1*(3): 256–270.

Rogers, C. (1951). *Client Centred Therapy*. London: Constable.

Rosenfeld, H. (1971). A clinical approach to the psychoanalytic theories of the life and death instincts: an investigation into the aggressive aspects of narcissism. *International Journal of Psychoanalysis, 51*:169–178.

*Rowan, J. (2001). *Ordinary Ecstasy: The Dialectics of Humanistic Psychology* (3rd edn). London: Brunner/Routledge.

*Russell, G. (1979). Bulimia nervosa: An ominous variant of anorexia nervosa. *Psychological Medicine, 9*: 429–448.

*Schore, A. (2001). The effects of early relational trauma on right brain development, affect regulation, and infant mental health. *Infant Mental Health Journal, 22*: 201–269.

*Searles, H. (1979). *Countertransference and Related Subjects: Selected Papers*. New York: International Universities Press.

*Seinfeld, J. (1991). *The Empty Core: An Object Relations Approach to Psychotherapy with the Schizoid Personality*. New Jersey: Aronson.

Sherwood, V., & Cohen, C. (1994). *Psychotherapy of the Quiet Borderline Patient,* Livingstone, NJ: Jason Aronson.

*Siegel, D. (1999) *The Developing Mind: Toward a Neurobiology of Interpersonal Experience*. New York: Guilford Press.

Stewart, I., & Joines, V. (Eds.) (2002). *Personality Adaptations: A New Guide to Human Understanding in Psychotherapy and Counselling*. Nottingham: Lifespace.

Stoltenberg, C. D., & Delworth, U. (1987). *Supervising Counselors and Therapists: A Developmental Approach*. San Francisco: Jossey-Bass.

Talbot, N. (1995). Unearthing shame in the supervisory experience. *American Journal of Psychotherapy, 49*(3): 338–349.

Tomkins, S. S. (1963). *Affect, Imagery and Consciousness: The Negative Affects* (Vol. 2). New York: Springer.

*Van der Kolk, B. (1989). The compulsion to repeat the trauma: re-enactment, revictimization and masochism. *Psychiatric Clinics of North America, 12*(2), 389–411.

Van der Kolk, B., & McFarlane, A. (1996). The black hole of trauma. In: *Traumatic Stress: The Effects of Overwhelming Experience on Mind, Body and Society.* New York: Guilford Press.

Van der Kolk, B., Van der Hart. O., & Burbridge. J. (1995). Approaches to the treatment of PTSD. In: S. Hobfoll & M. de Vries (Eds.), *Extreme Stress and Communities: Impact and Intervention* (NATO Asi Series. Series D, Behavioural and Social Sciences, Vol 80). Norwell, MA: Kluwer.

Ware, P. (1983). Personality adaptations. *Transactional Analysis Journal, 13*: 11–19

Wheeler, G. (1995). Shame in two paradigms of therapy. *British Gestalt Journal, 4*(2): 76–85.

Wheeler, G. (1997). Self and shame: a Gestalt approach. *Gestalt Review, 1*(3): 221–244.

Wilson, J. P., & Lindy, J. D. (1994). Empathic strain and countertransference. In: J. P. Wilson & J. D. Lindy (Eds.), *Countertransference in the Treatment of PTSD.* New York: Guilford Press.

Winnicott, D. W. (1945). Primitive emotional development. *International Journal of Psychoanalysis, 26*:137–143.

Winnicott, D. W. (1989). On the basis of sef in body. In: *Psychoanalytic Explorations.* Cambridge, MA: Harvard University Press.

Wolf, N. (1991). *The Beauty Myth: How Images of Beauty Are Used Against Women.* New York: Morrow.

Woodman, M. (1982). *Addiction to Perfection: The Still Unravished Bride.* Toronto: Inner City Books.

Wurmser, L. (1981). *The Mask of Shame.* Baltimore: Johns Hopkins University Press.

Yalom, I. (1980). *Existential Psychotherapy.* New York: Basic Books.

Yontef, G. M. (1993). *Awareness, Dialogue & Process.* New York: The Gestalt Journal Press.

Yontef, G. M. (1996). Gestalt Supervision. *British Gestalt Journal, 5*(2): 92–102.

INDEX